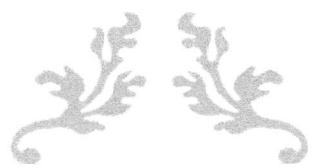

GOD IS!

Inner Outer Struggles

JEWELINE R. ANDREWS

KATRINA'S WORKS

PUBLISHING

LLC

Except for biblical verses and cited work, the words and phrases are exclusively those of the author's. No part of this book may be used or reproduced in any matter without permission, except in the case of brief quotations embodied in articles or reviews. All rights are reserved by the author.

ISBN-978-0692982983

ISBN-0692982981

God IS!

Inner Outer Struggles

Copyright © November 2017

Jeweline R. Andrews

Cover Design

by

Soul Sister Ink

Katrinasworks.com

FROM THE AUTHOR:

Amazingly I had a dream, a vision God said: "Go purchase a royal blue suit, hat, shoes and bag to match." I didn't follow up on my supernatural vision but couldn't forget it. So, I shared it with certain family members too hard to keep great things to myself. God reminded me of my vision a second time, I shared it with a woman of faith a former student of our former school, 'Wonder' who baby-sat for me back in the day said, "He desires you to walk in royalty." Today, my God given vision is reality clothe in the mind of Christ, apostle Paul wrote. "Put on the whole armor of God that you may be able to stand against the wiles of the devil. For we do not wrestle against flesh and blood, but against principalities, against powers against the rules of darkness of the age, against spiritual wickedness in high places." **Ephesians 6:11-12**. Amazing! The light is on blue skies changes color spiritual, physical, etc.

God changes not; great principles in life says, "Children, obey your parents in the LORD, for this is right. Honor your father and your mother, which is the first commandment with promise: That it may be well with you, and you may live long on earth." **Ephesians 6:1-3**. Dads have a charge to keep says. "And you, fathers, do not provoke your children to wrath, but bring them up in the training and admonition of the LORD." **Verse 4**. The purified Word trains His people. See **verses 5-6**. Even in struggles do it, obey and trust God: "With goodwill doing service, as to the LORD, and not to men, knowing that what-ever good anyone does, he will receive the same from the LORD, whether he is a slave or free." **Verses 7-8**. According, to the will of God the witness team obeyed Him, walked the streets together east, west, north and south unless hindered by reasons, because He knows all things.

Paul wrote moral principles wisdom from above, with pleasure I pass on again these things say. "And you masters do the same things to them, forbearing threatening; knowing that your Master also is in heaven, neither is there respect of persons with Him." **Ephesians 6:9**. Believers should act on, again, Paul says again in **Colossians 4:1-4,** "Masters, give your servants what is just and equal, knowing that you have a Master in heaven. Continue in prayer, and watch in the same with thanksgiving; meanwhile praying also for us, that God would open to us a door of utterance, to speak the mystery of Christ, for which I am also in chains, that I may make it manifest, as I ought to speak." Again, God introduced me to writing; I hope to express some great things I love likewise as did Paul. For example, as His witness, I confess the witness team delightedly use His works, acts and power to; "Walk in wisdom toward those who are outside, redeeming the time. Let your speech always be with grace, seasoned with salt, that you may know how you ought to answer each one." **Verses 5-6**. Most assuredly God is the glory. Many years later it is a miracle I witness in marketplaces, by phone, anytime, anyplace it is a pleasure in Him to just do it.

Paul made it plain to us what we must do says. "And take the helmet of salvation and the sword of the Spirit, which is the Word of God; praying always with all prayer, supplication for all the saints." **Ephesians 6:17-18**. A writer titled a song, "GOD IS Protector!" 'From the heart reaches the heart,' increase my confidence my first book, titled: *The way of Escape These Things. I prayed* for an editor in our hometown that would re-edit my God breathed book, Katrina Avant, an independent publisher/editor completed my second edition above in 2015. Secondly my second book title, God IS! *Inner Outer Struggles*, expresses one struggle end, a new one began. I pray that His truth will help others likewise, as someone like me: whether up, or down I know He's with me. Paul declared. "One God, Father of all, who is above all, through all, in you all. But to every one of us is given grace accordingly to the measure of the gift of Christ**." Ephesians 4:6-7**.

"Pilate said to Him, what is truth? And when he had said this, he went out again to the Jews and said to them. I find in Him no fault at all." **John 18:38.** Truth is that which is true, I continue to write the way of escape notable by choice, two-way paths. Good versus bad. Thirdly, my first chapter entitled, "Amazing Places Even in Struggles." "Then Pilate said, are You speaking to me? Do you not know I have the power to crucify You, and have power to release You? Jesus answered, you could have no power at all against Me unless it had been from above. Therefore, the one who delivered Me to you has the greater sin." **John 19:10-11**. Jesus said: "Because I tell you the truth, you do not believe Me." **John 8:45**. So, I pray for peace and truth instead of war: Apostle John wrote these things "Greeting to Gaius the elder to the beloved, Gaius whom I love in truth: I pray that you may prosper in all things and be in health, just as your soul prospers." **III John 1-2**. Fourthly, my second chapter is titled: "A Charge to Keep Even in Struggles."

Awesomely, by grace my third Chapter entitled, A Time to Shout Even in Struggles: in awe, Apostle John says, "For I rejoice greatly when brethren came and testified of the truth that is in you, just as you walk in the truth. I have no greater joy than to hear that my children walk in the truth." **Verse 3-4**. Praise God all of us are included; I dedicate my God spoken second book to Him inspired though Him, by Him, my precious family, extended family, and whosoever reads these things. Memories of my deceased family, friends in spirit, for, "GOD IS A Spirit." **John 4:24a**.

Awed-struck in Him I love the graceful song recorded in His Word say. "Then Moses and the children of Israel sang this song to the LORD, for He has triumphed gloriously! The horse and its rider He has thrown into the sea! The LORD is my strength and song. And has become my salvation. He is my God and I will praise Him: My father's God, and I will exalt Him." **Exodus 15:1-2.** Questions are: "Who is like unto You, O LORD, among the gods? Who is like You, glorious in holiness, Fearful in praises, doing wonders? You stretched out Your right hand; the earth swallowed them. You, in mercy have led forth the people who You have redeemed; You have guided them in Your strength to Your holy habitation." **Verses 11-13.**

How Awesome IS HE? Glorious in holiness, inspired, by it clearly great words we hear very little about today, yet Jesus is my personal inspiration, saved sanctified by the precious blood of Jesus Christ, who is fearlessly my Rock. I will pass it on again; tell it, and share awesomely. "For God so loved the world that He gave His only begotten Son, that whosoever believe in Him should not perish but have everlasting life." **John 3:16**. God made my case, because my fourth Chapter titled: East, West, North, South, All In Between. Awesomely, "God sent His Son into the world not to condemn the world, but the world through Him might be saved." **Verse 17**.

I attended some ladies meet and greet event, a young lady heard me say God breathe in my, spirit to write the book. So, a lady handed me a journal and four blank tablets, I continue to write. So, a young lady read my first book excitedly said to my face; she longed to write a book. So, if authors desire a publisher in our hometown, Katrina's Works Publishing's website e-mail information is at the closing of this book. I showed my first book to an expert who turned to my first chapter, he asked me what did I mean God breathed in my spirit? Abundantly it's on record: "And He breathed on them, and said Receive you the Holy Spirit:" **John 20:22b**.

      I received the Holy Spirit. In amazement, I revisited a certain church one Sunday morning, the word was out God healed their pastor who was sick in a coma. His wife and members prayed fervently for him. One Sunday he returned to church, I was in the building, the members shouted praises to God I joined in with them. He preached like he practiced Jesus teaches, saying. "But the Helper, the Spirit, whom the Father will send in My name, He will teach you all things, and bring all things to your remembrance all things that I said to you." **John 14:26**. Amazingly, he titled his sermon. 'If you Can Stand the Pull, He will Pull you out.' A young man, even before God formed him in his mom's belly, he grew up, struggles attacked him: called me his second mom, made a wall plaque for me said the words he penned on it tell his true story and mine say.

      "But God commended His love to us, while we were yet sinners, Christ died for us." **Romans 5:8**. Even today, I'm enriched, in the joy of God's divine love that demonstrates His grace say: "Much more than having now been justified by His blood, we shall be saved from the wrath through Him. For if when we were enemies, we were reconciled to God through, the death of His Son, much more having been reconciled, we shall be saved by His life." **Verses 9-10**. I agree Jesus justified by His blood. I consider a song titled, "How I Got Over." Again, mindfully aware. "Nicodemus said to Him, how can a man be born again when he is old? Can he enter a second time into his mother's womb and be born? Jesus answered. Most assuredly, I say to you, unless one is born of water and the

Spirit, he cannot enter into the kingdom of heaven." **John 3:4-5**.

Luke, a Gentile physician made the case to the world, I believe every word. Says, "But you shall receive power when the Holy Spirit has come upon you; and you shall be witnesses to Me in Jerusalem, and all Judah and Samaria, to the end of the earth." **Acts 1:8.** Glancing back, Wonder Gathering was held in the great city, Nashville TN. May 26-28, 2016, Memorial Day weekend; a genuine blessing. I offer special thanks to Dr. Willie Mae Peete, Mrs. Magnolia Smothers, great volunteers, all participants in my very own God breathed book. One asked, who would host Wonder Gathering next year? Dr. Peete and Mrs. Smothers walked a finished line dressed in famous black tuxedos approved by the two of them. So, two of us, agreed to host Wonder Gathering in West Memphis, AR. Memorial Day weekend May 25-26, 2017, two days, and nights reserved a Hugh place for the entire events to be held on here on Broadway.

I called Dr. Peete with the news, she said okay: two weeks later she called me; said Dr. Gloria Nixon Pone and Dr. Darrell Pone, former class, 1963, desired to host the event. Dr. Peete said she assisted the couple; most plans were setup and I agreed. So, Wonder Gathering was held in Fayetteville Georgia on Memorial Day weekend 2017. Glancing back, I move forward with intention to continue to write as our LORD grants utmost wisdom from above, and express great things He reveals to me to complete my second God breathe book, what a journey !

Reflections of life

In memory of our former classmate of Wonder High, class of 1961 Mrs. Gerline Dickson Mays, a hall of famous Board Member in the beginning of this famous event, *Wonder Gathering*. She served as a volunteer famously until sickness led to death. She was a faithful friend from third grade throughout her lifetime. May God rest her soul. Class of 1961 her entire family, friends, also her church home was Mount Vernon in Memphis in that she served famously till death. Moreover, my request I believe, sent from above that our school "Wonder" remain by name, for it is a wonder working miracle in memory the first black school in our city to God is the glory. Our school song is notable in my first book and second edition titled the way of escape these things.

Surprise! To us, find yourself in the *Wonder Gathering* group picture below. Some of you that were present had to leave early, etc. We missed you! And know you were awesomely present for the awed-inspired Gathering. May God continue to bless us more abundantly. So be it.

CHAPTER ONE

"Amazing Places Even in Struggles"

Song writers penned words of comfort to affirm God's love, I believe words from the Scripture such as a song entitled. "SWEET HOUR OF PRAYER," the writer wrote "In seasons of distress and grief, my soul has often found relief." The peace of God comforts me; inner outer struggles cause me pain at times, yet they help me grow stronger in the LORD. For example, I believe the word consider is an action verb from above to help me think and obey when He calls my name; wakes me up, is greater than the day before. Because the writer's last word says, "This robe of flesh I'll drop, and rise to seize the everlasting prize." Comfort me to know these things.

A question was asked at a meeting I attended, should "Black Lives Matter? All lives matter to God more than I know. A song writer penned, "At the Cross," I understand abundantly who said, "I am a worm." **Psalm 22:6a**. David God's anointed king struggled, but He anointed him. A young man prayed at their meeting to the God of his weary years, like tested severely. Yet Job a man tried, tested, convicted inward outwardly his friend accused him falsely said. "You have not given the weary water to drink, and you have withheld bread from the hungry. But the mighty man possessed the land, and the honorable man dwelt in it. You have sent widows away empty. And the strength of the fatherless was crushed." **Job 22:7-9**. I believe, the young black man found his answer. So, it happened; a tomb; a grave could not hold Jesus, and His great evangelist wrote the cause. "He is risen." **Mark 16:6b**. David struggled yet he didn't quit, he testified said.

"Blessed is he who considers the poor. The LORD will deliver in the time of trouble. The LORD will preserve him and keep him alive. And he will be blessed on earth: You will not deliver him to the will of his enemies. You will sustain him on his sickbed." **Psalm 41:1-3**. **See verses 4-8**. A song writer penned, "What a Friend We Have in Jesus." So, when friends forsake us, black lives matter it is all I know smile! David recorded. "Even my own familiar friend in whom I trusted: Who ate my bread has lifted-up his heel against me. But You, O LORD, be merciful to me, and raise me up, that I may repay them. By this I know that You are pleased with me, for, my enemy does not triumph over me, as for me: You uphold me in my integrity, and set me before Your face forever." **Psalm 41:9-12**. Integrity is honesty, strengths firm character, hold to it. "Blessed be the God of Israel from ever-lasting to everlasting Amen." **Verse 13**. Consider God's infinite love even being black He created black nights, **Genesis 1:2**; the light **1:3**, darkness and light **1:4** both **1:5**. God made black horses **Revelation 6:5**, white horses revelation **19:11**. Plus I can't forget integrity is truthfulness Solomon said, "A feast is made for laughter: And wine makes merry: but money answers everything." **Ecclesiastes 10:19**. Make sure money isn't our idol, integrity wise.

So, what matters to God, dominion power works says. "Set your mind on things above, not on earth." **Colossians 3:2**. Amazingly places even in struggles all lives matter to the old, to young millennials men women rich or poor. "Jesus said to him: Friend, why have you come? Then they came and laid hands on Jesus. And suddenly one of those who were with Jesus stretched out his hand and drew his sword, struck the servant of the high priest, and cut off his ear." **Matthew 26:50-51**. Even so, a man acted on his mission one way. "But Jesus said to him: Put your sword in its place, for all who take the sword will perish by the sword. Or do you think that I cannot now pray to My Father, and He will provide me with more than twelve legions of angels? How then could the Scriptures be fulfilled, that it must happen thus? **Verses 52-54**.

Many people especially black young boys' search for love, grow up without a fathers' tender kindnesses to teach them how to be real men. I observed the Word say; "In that same hour Jesus said to the multitude: Have you come out, as against a robber, with swords and clubs to take Me?" I sat daily with you, teaching in the temple and you did not seize Me. But all this was done that the Scriptures of the prophets might be fulfilled." **Matthew 26: 55-56**. My only son said he and his family attended a church, in hope, the pastor would teach him to be a man. I shared his words with a lawyer he was angry. I realize, even the truth hurts, I try to come clean with Jesus who said. "But seek you first the kingdom of God and His righteousness and all these things will be added to you." **Matthew 6:33**. Jesus doesn't give up on anyone black lives matter.

I'm nothing without Jesus and confess by grace He sent a message from above abundantly says. "Sanctify them through Your truth, Your Word is truth." **John 17: I7**. As a believer, I continue to search the Word daily it pays off in full Jesus said. "As You sent Me into the world, I also sent them into the world. And for their sakes I sanctify Myself, that they may be sanctified by the truth." **Verses 18-19**. The way for me to escape bad habits such as saying; I can't do this, or that, rightly. Suppose our LORD'S first disciples likewise refused His offer to obey the One that keeps us breathing. God planned His purpose, a King for His kingdom. Jesus called His disciples by name all twelve of them, "He gave them power against unclean spirits to cast them out, and heal all matter of disease." Revisit **Matthew**

10:1-4; see verses 5-40. I could make a list of things they did right verses, wrong, includes me, as results, Jesus makes no errors fast forwarded. A tax collector excelled and followed Jesus, an expert, who probably charged much tax on the outcast people. Jesus made a charge said. "And whosoever gives one of these little ones a cup of cold water in the name of a disciple, assuredly, I say to you, he shall by no means lose his reward." **Matthew 10:42**. Those who obey God in His kingdom do them purposely.

For example, David, wrote, "Sing praises to the LORD, that dwells in Zion; declare among the people. When He avenges blood, He remembers them; He does not forget the cry of the humble. Have mercy on me, O LORD! Consider my troubles from those hate me: You who lift me up from the gates of hell." **Psalm 9:11-13**. Works and acts of God, verse 14-20 especially verse 15. David didn't follow mad angry people as it is happening today. He knew one would reap and sow So, He quickens my spirit, my breath is the precious gift of life from God, so then **Psalm 23:1-6** hangs on my south bedroom wall I revisit daily, it happened suddenly while rereading. "Surely goodness and mercy shall follow me all the days of my life:" Verse 6a, I can't see my back yet God's got my back a priceless gift quickens my spirit to move me forward observe these words.

"As the deer pants for the water brooks. So, my soul thirsts for You, O God, for the living God. When shall I come and appear before God? My tears have been my food day and night. While they continually say to me where is your God? When I remember these things. I pour out my soul within me." **Psalm 42:1-4a**. The sons of Korah worked as temple musician assistants illustrated true eloquent love of God to the world, deer's must have water, every living thing need water to survive. At times, I look back, so thankful to God I'm not condemn. The sons of Korah wrote like they heard me use says. "For I use to go with the multitude; I went with them to the house of God. With the voice of joy and praise. With a multitude that kept a pilgrim feast. Why are you cast down, O my soul? And why are you disquieted within me? **Verses 4b-5a**.

I used to run the race for anyone that needed a ride, east, west, north and south until it wore me out doing my best of services as unto our God. At that time, my husband was disable fourteen years, five of those years I was trained to used my knees to lift him, as caregiver. Nursing homes didn't enter our minds, likewise the sons of Korah purposely says, I copy well as act on says. "Hope in God, for I will yet praise Him for the help of my countenance." **Verse 5b**. As a noun Countenance show facial expression, happy, sad, in struggles or weary. I glanced in a mirror my face expressed pain, I hopped on my right foot, and my knee racked with great pain. So, I opened my Bible my eyes fell on **Luke 7**. A Roman soldier demonstrated love for his beloved servant who was sick. Fast forwarded the man said to Jesus. "But say a word and my servant will be healed." **7:7b**. So, I trust His Word and said Healer 'say a word.' serving God pays of, for real.

A few days later, I walked instead of hoped, and leaped for joy God healed me. The Spirit reminded me of my dream in capital letters HEALED; He awaken me early one morning, I penned in my first book the way of escape these things. For example, countenance. as a verb mean to encourage, or give consent. A writer's song encourages me today titled, I believe "Put it All in His Hand. Big This That Little that," My GOD is Bigger than the world He's got it all things in His hand. When things go wrong as they sometimes will His revelations good, or bad I doubt self, not Him, the sons Korah put it all in His hands says. "O my

God, my soul is cast down within me; Therefore, I remember You from the land of Jordan, from the heights of Hermon. From the Hill Mizar. Deep calls unto deep at the noise of your waterfalls. And your waves and billows have gone over me." **Psalm 42: 6-7**. So, likewise I "Put it all in His hand."

"Hope in God." A friend shared with me whenever he felt blessed, things would happen to snatch away his joy. He struggled for days all alone. I shared with him, the same thing happened to me, for, the devil works like that, evil spirits show up dressed to kill, steal and destroy John 10:10a. but the story doesn't end here, Jesus says. "I have come that they may have life that they may have it more abundantly." **10b**. I consider God's promise say. "For He, Himself has said, I will never leave you nor forsake you. "**Hebrews 13:5b**. Jesus will do the same thing for anyone. A song writer knew and titled it, "NEVER ALONE." The writer is unknown. A taste of the first verse say: "I've seen the lighting flashing: And heard the thunder roll, I've felt sin's breakers dashing, which tried to conquer my soul, I've heard the voice of my Savior, He bid me still to fight on-- He promised: Never to leave me:" conquers my soul. Never is a good adverb to keep me free from the love of money, yet its' no secret God knows I need some to use it, not allow it to use me.

I had a sudden flashed back, that blessed me delightedly. Moreover, the sons say. "The LORD will command His loving-kindness in the daytime, and in the night His song shall be with me, a prayer to the God of my life. I will say to God my Rock, why have You forgotten me? Why do I go mourning because of the oppression of the enemy?" **Psalm 42:8-9**. Great questions are asked the sons wrote "As with a breaking of my bones: My enemies approached me: While they say to me all day long, where is your God? Why are you cast down, O my soul? And why are you disquieted within me? Hope in God: For I will yet praise Him: The help of my countenance and my God." **Verses 10-11**. Even so struggles float on. "For these things had to be done the Scriptures had to be fulfilled: Not one of His bones shall be broken. Again, another Scripture says: They shall look of Him whom they pierced." **John 19:36-37**. He guards all His bones: Not one of them is broken evil shall the wicked." **Psalm 34:20-21b**.

The sons of Korah said "Vindicate me, O God; And plead my cause against an ungodly nation; Oh, deliver me from deceitful and unjust man! For You are the God of my strength; why do you cast me off? Why do I go mourning because of the oppression of the enemy? Oh, send me Your light and truth!" **Psalm 43:1-3a**. The writers of Psalm 42 & 43 are the authors: means to avenge, defend, exonerate and grant us freedom in life, amazing places even in struggles. My dear readers the Word is the strength of my life. I had no idea writing would keep me in such great company, even so God knew it. As results, I'm encouraged exceedingly glad, despite dilemmas undesirable unwanted inner outer struggles; yet my God given Joy truly exceeds my struggles humbly by faith down deep in my heart, I believe is very good vindications.

I sent a copy of my first God given book to a woman of faith, close to my heart she critiqued it was good feedback. Although, God makes no mistakes, I make errors daily, even so not purposely. He said write the book it took me years to start on my assignment; again, I couldn't escape His orders any longer. So, the woman of faith sent me some authors work, I did not understand, so, an expert said we know it's the message that counts. More abundantly, I am determined to write since tests and trials help me to pass on redeeming the time by faith in Him a palmist report said. "My soul faints for Your salvation. But I hope in Your Word. My eyes fail, searching Your Word. Saying, when will You comfort me? **Psalm 119:81-82**.

Looking back on East Central Arkansas Economic Development Corp, which at that time was an agency that housed aging program for seniors 60+ and other components. It consisted of eight senior sites, adult daycare and Marion kitchen, in three sites, Crittenden, Cross and St. Francis counties. So, I volunteered to help serve the elderly. The agency had an open position, I applied for it, the executive hired me as data clerk. The exec told a site director he knew well when my supervisor retires he would hire me as aging director was impressive. I knew God was at work it is written, "Do not boast about tomorrow." **Proverbs 27:1a**. I was interviewed by three experts of the agency that approved of my character. So, my supervisor passed away, God rest her soul; the exec that was going to hire me, passed away God rest his soul also I was flabbergasted.

A new executive was hired; like my first exec predicted, the new one hired me: but I rejected his offer, named someone, to hold the position. A deacon and, an elder lady unless immensely hindered I picked her up twelve years for Sunday school: the two of them said I gave up my position was abundantly true. Because, the person, the exec hired at my request, returned to his old position. The exec said I had a choice if I reject his offer, as aging director, for three counties I could go home, he didn't need me! I needed to work, and accepted the position penned a taste of this in my first and second edition, the way to escape these things. Solomon said, "to every- there is a season." **Ecclesiastes 3:1**. So, I make mention of Joseph's struggles notable to me, because, God reminded me He didn't forget Joseph nor did his biology daddy, for example.

I called my first publisher checked on my first book after she had it for a year and four months. She couldn't find my flask disk I saved my book on. She said oh yes, the escape! She said wait.

So, I waited but didn't return to her phone, waited God said hang up the phone I obeyed blessed to know His voice. He said so plainly I didn't forgot Joseph, nor did his biology dad I received the revelation and shared it with my family. The reason I know the peace of God flowed down my spine, the Word says. "But when the time of the promise drew nigh, which God had sworn to Abraham, the people grew and multiplied in Egypt, till another king arose which did not know Joseph. This man dealt treacherously with our people, and oppressed our fore-fathers, making them expose their babies so that they might not live." **Acts 7:17-19: verses 20-29.**

I recall amazing places even in struggles likewise as it happened. Luke a Gentile physician recorded, Moses lead the people seen in Exodus 3. Luke wrote. "And when forty years had passed, an angel of the LORD appeared to him in a flame of fire in a bush, in the wilderness of Mount Sinai. When Moses saw it, he marveled at the sight; and drew near to observe, the voice of the LORD came to him." **Acts 7:30-31.** These great sights came to me in a vision from the book of Exodus; in which reminds me of the way to escape these things I will my vision. Miracles happen especially whenever we listen to hear from God from His Word amazingly.

Meanwhile, Aging program networked with Four Season yearly we worked planned amazing annual tours for seniors, those who lived alone loved to travel, affordably, east, west, north or south the journey was incredible greater yearly. The seniors chose to visit Dr. Martin Luther King Jr. Center for Social Change the trip was breathtakingly like 'fire in a bush' written above.

I picked up a paper plaque, a verse I recorded in my first book and second edition says, "Everybody can be great, because anybody can serve. You don't have to make your subject and verbs agree to serve." So, it is an amazing journey. The seniors had amazing abundant blessings every year, Four Seasons tours plan the best sights in every city like five days, nights included. We traveled in daylight, relaxed in different cities at night in hotels that were excellent memoirs meanwhile.

We made it home safely I misplaced my plaque. But, the four of us from the church we served, enrolled in a Bishop, wife workshop in Atlanta, so, we spilt, the cost, and returned to the city attended a workshop informatively great; so, then we returned home safe. I found my plaque the words inspire me continuously inside out, because, another sentence written on my plaque that says, "You only need a heart full of grace a soul generated by love." Rev. Martin King Jr." More abundantly, Jesus said, "Greater love has no one than this, than to lay down one's life for his friends: You are my friend if you do whatever I command," **John 15:13-14:**

God is Creator, Ruler, the Government rest on the shoulder of Christ, **see Isaiah 9:6-7**. Jesus made a charged says "No longer do I call you servants, for a servant does not know what his master is doing; but I have called you friends. For all things that I heard from My Father I have made known to you. You did not choose Me, but I chose you and appointed you that you should go and bear fruit, and your fruit should remain." **John 15:15-16a**. Jesus points to prosperity says "Whatever you ask the Father in My name He will give you. These things I command you, that you love one another." **Verses 16b-17**. A song writer penned; "No greater Love."

Moreover, a personal relationship with our Father I believe remains abundantly, the apostle John wrote, Jesus said. "As many as I love, I rebuke and chasten. Therefore, be zealous and repent." **Revelation 3:19**. Zealous mean, zeal in that gives one great energy to make it personal. Jesus energizes me with the joy of the LORD I believe to keep writing. Repent, means being genuinely sorry for sins I use the Word continuously to forgive **Mark 11:22-26**. An iron black plaque hangs on my south kitchen wall a writer penned my genuine long-term goals overwhelm says. "LORD fill my mouth with worth-while stuff and nudge me when I've said enough." I ask God to test my words, for I can't take them back, whether good, or bad; moreover years-ago even before I left home His presence was noticeable in my house I praised Him abundantly.

Although, at that time, the building was very small; we were packed together like peas in the shell ready to burst open at harvest time. As results, members praised God together, genuinely. So it happened; a deacon who continually serve today asked me to read the secretary's report in her absence one Sunday morning. I leaped to my feet, knees wobbled, voice cracked, hands shook like leaves on a tree, I was afraid but read the announcements as I trembled. Although my mind fell on Jonah a prophet of God whose purpose was to show the extent of God's grace. I remember conspicuously the Word says, "Now the Word of the LORD came to Jonah the son of Amittal, saying: Arise, go the Nineveh, that great city and cry out against it: for their wickedness has come up before Me. But Jonah arose to flee to Tarshish from the presence of the LORD.

He went down to Joppa, and found a ship going to Tarshish from the presence of the LORD." **Jonah 1:1-3**. The prophet disobeyed, but he didn't escape his God spoken assignment.

"But the LORD sent out a great wind on the sea, and there was a mighty tempest on the sea, so that the ship was about to be broken up. Then the mariners were afraid, and every man cried out to his god, and threw the cargo that was in the ship into the sea, to lighten the load. But Jonah had gone down into the lowest parts of the ship, lain down and was fast asleep." **Verses 4-5**. A lesson learned, the captain had an assignment, an expert had to act like it. "So, the captain came to him and said to him: What do you mean, sleeper? Arise, call on your God; perhaps your God will consider us, so, that we may not perish." **Verse 6.** A song, I believe says, "God's Going to Carry the Heavy Load." **See verses 7-16.**

Again it is right to consider Jonah testified saying, "Then I said, I have been cast out of Your sight: Yet I look again toward Your holy temple. The waters surrounded me even to my soul; the deep closed around me; weeds were wrapped around my head." **Jonah 2:4-5**. God works, He doesn't need our help to get people to obey Him; see **verses 6-9a.** For, "Salvation is of the LORD." **Verse 9b.** In the process years-ago in the church I serve, today I taught the Book of Jonah in the adult women class instructed to do it.

I listen obeyed the Holy Spirit then the deacon, I finished teaching, my mind returned to me from God. I asked a teacher/ deacon who attended college with a Bible in his hand; if I left of anything from the book of Jonah? He said nothing. During that time, the deacon, taught our adult women class said, no test, no testimony even so, amazing places even in struggles continues.

Moreover, whether I like it or not God test me daily, so, truth inspires me even more, because I struggled and thrive to move forward. And try to imagine the way it feels if a strong east wind blows in my back gets my attention, I feel the wind yet I can't see it. Later, a teacher said he was going to teach the Book of Jonah I praised God shared with him I was writing a taste about him even before lessons appeared in the Sunday school commentary God does things before time. I recall a preacher that married my husband and I, said he wouldn't question my absence from church, for I knew before time, the lessons, at that time, I had no commentary! God is my witness; I don't boast but celebrate His many miracles. Although I can't see the wind I feel its presence same as I hear the Holy Spirit my Helper speak to me. The Book of Jonah is instilled in my God given memory I prayed, and fasted the year of 2015, moreover to refresh myself in my down time deep in my soul to obey the Spirit.

The Book of Jonah is a must read I believe. "So, Jonah arose and went to Nineveh, that great city, and preached to it according to the word of the LORD. Now Nineveh was a great city, a three-day journey in exact. And Jonah began to enter the city on the first day's walk. Then he cried out said: Yet forty days, and Nineveh shall be overthrown!" **Jonah 3:3-4**. That was miraculously the way God used and sent Jonah to preach.

"So, the people of Nineveh believed God, and proclaimed a fast, and put on sackcloth, from the greatest to the least of them." **Verses 5; See verses 6-7**. And it happened they obeyed says. "But let man and beast be covered with sackcloth, and cry mightily to God; yes, let everyone turn from his evil way and from the violence that is in his hands." Verse 8 the king testified said. "Who can tell if God will turn and relent, and turn away from His fierce anger, so that we may not perish? Then God saw their works, that they turned from their evil way and God relented from the disaster that He had said He would bring upon them, and He did not do it." **Verses 9-10**.

Relent means to repent change one's mind forgive; like God forgives us How Great is He? Jonah's anger at God's appointed time, he debated it with God mightily. Revisit four chapters see His works and acts. Today, who can tell about these evil things we witness now? It is written remember Solomon, says "When the righteous are in authority, the people rejoice: But when a wicked man rules, the people groan." **Proverbs 29:2**. It's true. Evil versus good.

A psalmist wrote: "For their sake He remembers His covenant, and relented according, to the multitude of His mercies." **Psalm 106:45.** Immensely, my grands loved to make mud pies in my front yard, but at clean up time no volunteers. Saturday mornings paid off, no school. They got the Word, "Thy rod and thy staff they comfort me." **Psalm 23:4b**. Works, they used their God given five senses and missed thy rod of correction. The above words paid off and I forgave them.

History lessons are profitable to all people; I should have listened more abundantly. Paul said: "Moreover, brethren, I would not that you should be ignorant, how that all our fathers were under the cloud all passed through the sea. All of them were baptized unto Moses in the cloud and in the sea. And did all eat the same spiritual meat; and all drank the same spiritual Rock that followed them, and that Rock was Christ." **I Corinthians 10:1-4. A** song writer wrote: "Rock of Ages, Cleft for me, let me hide myself in thee." The Word directs our path saying. "But with most of them God was not pleased, for they were overthrown in the wilderness. Now these things became our examples to the intent that we should not lust after evil things as they all so lusted." **Verses 5-6**. Lust is my earthen natural desire to comfort my flesh.

"No temptation has overtaken you except such as is common to man; God Is, faithful, who will not allow you to be tempted beyond what you are able, but with the temptation will also make the way of escape, that you may be able to stand." **Verse 13**. It hangs on my south wall, since November 8, 2007. It is informative, the way to escape these things saying, "Therefore, my beloved, flee from idolatry." verse 14. Paul said, "I speak as to wise men, judge for yourselves what I say. The cup of blessing which we bless, is it not the communion of the body of Christ? The bread which we break, is it not the communion of the body of Christ? For we, though many, are one bread and one body for we are partakers of that one bread." **Verses 15-17**. All lives matter to God, some black men are hated same as Jesus yet; we are partakers together, one hell, one heaven choose. God is faithful He doesn't tempt us. The song writer got it right, "Yield Not to Temptation."

As a democrat by choice, politicians ought to work to serve all Americans; march for Civil Rights, since government is good. 'Watch the space.' Floods, fires and earthquakes warn us. Democrats from Washington D.C. sent me surveys, asking who should run for a Republican president. I responded on the survey by asking, who is qualified to run for president? From the survey, many people ran for the highest position in 2016, but I quoted a famous senator who said, "I'M WITH HER."I was incredibly pleased with the senator's remarks.

In 2015, I penned on a survey, if congress agreed together to vote on a bill to raise all adult's wages to $15 an hour, with full-time work benefits and employer's agree, I believe laborers would not need food stamps to feed their families. Democrats know these things. Also I believe companies would increase a hundred-fold in their own businesses with both parties prospering together. I find amazing places even is struggles moving forward.

At that time, as an aging director at East Central Agency, a taste of my own true story, might help experts likewise. When raises were offered to me, if my staff did not received increases in pay, no raises were given out at all; Jesus declared it. "And as you would that men should do to you, do you also to them likewise." **Luke 6:31**. The golden rule works. I wrote on the demo survey, run the race Hillary. Paul asked, "Do you not know that those who run in a race all run, but one receives the prize? And everyone who competes for the prize is temperate in all things. Now they do it to obtain a perishable crown, but we for an imperishable crown." I Corinthians 9:**24-25.** I believe **Genesis 1:26-31,** in the year 2016, God promoted a woman for president of U.S.A. I invested in the evidence, "And Adam called his wife's name; Eve, the mother of all living. Also for Adam and his wife the LORD God made tunics of skin, and clothed them. Then the LORD said; Behold, the man has become like one of US, to know good and evil. **Genesis 3:20-22.**

My confidence is in God alone. He made the case. I'm no Politian, but I believe Hillary had to run for president again in 2016, because I believe inner outer struggles made her incredibly stronger. Even so, history repeats itself. As a citizen, I appreciate our God, and government. **Romans 13,** I wrote in my third chapter, Paul encouraged self by saying, "Therefore, I run thus: not with uncertainty. Thus, I fight: not as one that beats the air. But I discipline my body, bring it into subjection, lest, when I have preached to others, I myself should be disqualified." **I Cor. 9: 26-27**. So, thoughts of faithful women leaped in my mind that were confident; assured of God's divine love.

    Abundantly, I refer to my Bible to debate my case and get my feelings hurt at times. Yet, I try a little tenderness; woman of faith are partakers. God used Paul to make the case saying, "I commend to you Phoebe our sister, who is a servant of the church in Cenchrea, that you might receive her in the LORD in a manner worthy of the saints, and assist her in whatever business she has need of you: for indeed she has been a helper of many and of myself also." **Romans 16:1-2**. God in my witness at times. I make these things personal and rethink souls I led to Christ to celebrate Him; give God the glory. As did Paul saying, "Greet Phoebe and Aquila, my fellow workers in Christ, who risk their own necks for life to whom not only I give thanks, but all the churches of the Gentiles. Likewise greet the church that is in their houses." **Verses 3-5**. Abundantly, as witnesses and missionaries back in the day, our mission president assigned us to pray in our houses for last names A-Z. Paul got it; my hope is renewed.

    As a friend of God, life goes on. For the record, there is more. I commend Hillary to this day, as a witness to serve others also. I believe she is a friend of our **LORD**. Amazing places, even in struggles that's life. It is not fake news. Where there is life there is hope. Tent builders work together not just as family members only. I am thankful for all laborers, because it is not about me at all. I just try to obey our infinite God and denounce hate as it creeps up. Paul said, "Greet Mary, who also labored much with us." **Verse 6**.

    Hillary labored much and continues to serve after a walk in the woods with her dog. The presence of God was needful. She had to return to serve. It isn't over yet. Who said, 'watch the space'? Notable two-way choices, Paul says, "Now I urge you, brethren, note those who cause divisions and offenses avoid divisive contrary to the doctrine which you learned, and avoid, for there are some that do not serve our LORD Jesus Christ 7.

Therefore, I commend the Obamas who helped Hillary which reminds me what God said, in my kitchen four days before Election Day, Obama would be our 44th president, God is my witness. Again, I shared it with early morning worshipers, my former pastor and the members who were present. I penned in my first and second edition, titled, *The Way of Escape These Things*. At that time my fourteen-year-old granddaughter, unexpectedly interviewed me. She later signed up for the Air Force, and was accepted. She asked what did I mean 'the way of escape these things?' Abundantly surprised, I said God breathed in my spirit two verses Peter says, "Whereby are given unto us exceeding great and precious promises: by these you might be partakers of the divine nature having escaped the corruption that is in the world through lust." **II Peter 1:4.** Secondly, Paul recorded five words that says "Command and teach these things." **I Timothy 4:11**, abundantly.

My granddaughter replied, "Granny you love using the word abundantly." It means over flow, too much, wealthy, rich. We were abundantly on one accord. I yearn for God's approval. I just want to obey Him. Yet, struggles are like weights in a gym, too heavy to pick up, yet they make me strong when I'm weak. In likeness, God sends a Word like a text message on my cell phone; like trees planted by the water's edge strengths its roots to grow strong. So, Apostle John may have been a math expert saying, "And there are three that bear witness on earth, the Spirit; the water; and the blood, and these three agree as one. If we receive the witness of men, the witness of God is Greater; for this is the Spirit of God which He has testified of His Son." **I John 5:8-9**.

I make errors, don't count me out my name is written in the Book of life manifested with the knowledge and assurance throughout His Word seen in v**erses 10-12**. God hold the key.

"These things, I have written to you who believe in the name of the Son of God, that you may know that you have eternal life, and that you may continue to believe in the Son of God. Now this is the confidence that we have in Him that if we ask anything according to His will, He hears us. And it we know that He hears us, whatever we ask, we know we have the petitions that we have asked of Him." **Verses 13-14.** I'm near the end of my first chapter; believers have the right to petition or request respectfully as partakers in Christ Jesus the King of all glory says. "If anyone sees his brother sin a sin which does not lead to death, he will ask, and He will give him life for those who commit sin NOT leading to death. I do not say that he shall pray about that." **Verses 15-16**.

Beware of fake news. Petition the throne of His grace seek His Word daily. "All unrighteousness is sin, and there is a sin not leading to death." **I John 5: 17**. Resist falsehoods. Quiet time in Him works if one knows the truth reject liars. "And we know that whosoever is born of God does not sin, but he who has been born of God keeps himself. And the wicked one does not touch him. We know that we are of God, and the whole world lies under the wicked one." **Verse 18**. A young lady said a man said Jesus was a trick; I asked what book was he reading? She didn't know. Someone said to me, "please yourself, one is pleased." Here is what I know see verse 20, because, fake news cause fear, "Little children, keep yourselves from idols. Amen." **Verse 21.**

Nicodemus acknowledge Jesus; explained to him for the world to know. "That which is born of flesh is flesh, and that which is born of the Spirit is spirit." John 3:6. I believe Jesus taught Nicodemus a way to escape tradition, which is a culture passed down to generations, to another an oral opinion, of belief also it is deceptive, resist it I don't depend on human traditions. Jesus said, "Do not marvel that I say to you, you must be born again. The wind blows where it wishes you hear the sound of it, but you cannot tell where it comes from and where it goes so in everyone who is born of the Spirit." **Verses 7-8.** To make chapter one plain is personal to me, its' no secret "Nicodemus answered and said to Him: How can these things be? Jesus answered and said to him. Are you a teacher of Israel, and do not know these things?" **John 3: 9-10.** The rich man's questions touched my heart, for he just didn't know Jesus, even as a teacher over His chosen people. I believe he humbled self to meet and greet a Man name Jesus, it worked openly.

Trees are said to be the strongest plants with thick wooden trunks, branches and leaves often with edible delicious fruit available for anyone. Question is, suppose all trees on earth, branches, vines, and leaves wither up. What would Jesus say? "I Am the vine, you are the branches, He who abide in Me and I in him bears much fruit: for without me you can do nothing. If anyone does not abide in Me, he is cast out as a branch and is withered: and they gather them in the fire, and they are burned. If anyone abide in Me and My Word abide in you, you will ask what you desire and you shall have it." **John 15:5-6.** The key fit the lock perfectly as do vine and branches; "If you abide in Me, and My words abide, you will ask what you desire and it shall be done for you." **Verse 7**. I cannot even imagine life without Jesus breathe of life, comes from Him saying, "By this My Father is glorified, that you bear much fruit. As the Father loved me, I also have loved you: abide in My love. If you keep My commandments and abide in His love. These things have I spoken to you, that my joy may be full. This is the commandment, that you love one another as I have loved you." **John 15:8b-12**. Notably, love flows from the Spirit, our Helper.

Paul made it clear examine these things says; "Though you might have ten thousand instructors in Christ, yet you do not have many fathers; for in Jesus Christ I have begotten you through the gospel**." I Corinthians 4:15**. God is glorified amazing places in struggles. "For the kingdom of God is not in Word but in power. What do you want? Shall I come to you with a rod, or in love with the spirit of gentleness?" **Verse 20**. My choice, a summary near the end of chapter one says. "Having the breastplate of righteousness: and having shod your feet with the preparation of the gossip of peace. Above all, taking the shield of faith." **Ephesians 6:14b-16a.**

John penned Jesus said. "I know your works that you are neither cold or hot: I could wish you were cold or hot. So then, because you are lukewarm, neither cold or hot, I will vomit you out of my mouth." **Revelation 3:15-16.** Therefore, revisit **I Peter 5:1-4**. Summarized it is saying, "Likewise, younger people, submit yourselves to your elders. Yes, all of you be submissive to one another, and be clothed with humility, for God resist the proud: But gives grace to the humble." Could a certain Congress woman capture young millenniums attention 'clothe with humility resist, the proud? As results, Peter's hit record gives us about six instructions says, "Humble yourselves therefore under the mighty hand of God that he may exalt you in due time: casting all your care upon him; for He cares for you. Be sober, be vigilant; because your adversary the devil, as a roaring lion, walks about seeking whom he may devour." **Verses 6-8**. For don't stop here there is more of the same thing works in Him through Him for Him says.

"Resist him steadfast in the faith. Knowing that the same sufferings are experienced by your brotherhood in the world: but may the God of all grace who called us to His eternal glory by Jesus Christ after you have suffered a while: perfect establish, strengthen, settle you." **Verses 9-10**. Perfected love is: "To Him be the glory, and dominion, forever and ever Amen." **Verse 11.** Observe a little tenderness. "By Silvanus, our faithful brother as I consider him, I have written briefly, exhorting, and testifying that this is the true grace of God which you stand. She who is in Babylon, elect together with you, greets you; and so, does Mark my son. Greet one another with a kiss of love. Peace to you all who are in Christ Jesus Amen." **Verses 12-14**. The way to escape these things show amazing places even in struggles just resist the devil.

These things point to, the LORD of lords, the Divine One says: "Behold, a king will reign in righteousness. And princes will rule with justice. A man will be as a hiding place in the wind. And a cover from the tempest. As rivers of water in a dry place, as the shadow of a great rock in a weary land. The eyes of those who see will not be dim. And the ear of those who hear will listen." **Isaiah 32:1-3**. Great is our King who listens to hear us? Agur's wise words say, "Every Word of God is pure, He is a shield to those who put their trust in Him." **Proverbs 30:5**. So, an anonymous psalmist recorded: "Our soul waits for the LORD; He is our help and shield. For our heart shall rejoice in Him, because we have trusted in His holy name. Let Your mercy be upon us. just as we hope on you."

Psalm 33:20-22. David recorded, "I will wait for You his Strength. For "God is our defense" **Psalm 59:9**. Look down see verse 11. David wrote about the shield again says, "O God, behold our shield: And look upon the face of Your anointed." **Psalm 84:9**.

David shared the shield of faith and the anointed of God, **Psalm 23:5b**, "Thou anointed my head with oil." **23:5b**. So, I anoint my head daily reread the above chapter pays off. Amazing places in struggles, "Says, Touch not mine anointed ones, and do my prophets so harm." **105:15**. So, "Every Word of God is pure, He is a shield to those who put their trust in Him."

Back in the day, members showed love and immense kindness toward one another; clicks were few, prayer, worship, praise and honor to God was immense. Paul wrote. "Your body is the temple of the Holy Spirit who is in you." **I Corinthians 6:19b**. John recorded, "He was in the world, and the world was made through Him, and the world did not know Him. He came to His own and His own did not receive Him. But as many as received Him, to them He gave the right to become the children of God, to those who believe in His name." **John 1:10-12**. I believe God.

Even beyond measure, struggles and tears, John's record helps me greatly. "Who were born, not of the flesh, nor of the will of man, but of God. And the Word became flesh and dwelt among us, and we beheld His glory as of the only begotten of the Father, full of grace and truth." **Verses 13-14**. Father, Son, Holy Spirit, believers are inseparable in which is the Gospel truth. Years later, the church I love, financially wise, in every way I helped build it, life center class rooms, etc. I left the building to work on my God given assignment. Time flew by quickly, I didn't keep up with the time in His presence it wasn't necessary Paul got it and me to, says, "Jesus Christ Himself, the chief cornerstone, in whom the whole building, being fitted together, grow into a holy temple in the LORD, in whom you are being built together for a dwelling place of God in the Spirit." **Ephesians 2:20b-22**, Years later it was great. God tested me exceedingly hard.

I shared with my pastor, at that time it was hard; he said if it was easy, it probably wasn't God given, so he looked me in the face, called my name said obey God I accepted his advice. I recall the apostles were tested in **Acts 5:22-28**. "But Peter and the other disciples said: We ought to obey God rather than men. The God of our fathers raised up Jesus who you murdered by hanging on a tree. Him God has exalted to His right hand to be Prince and Savior, to give repentance to Israel and the forgiveness of sins." **Acts 5:29-31**. The evidence is notable it says. "And we are witnesses to these things, and so is the Holy Spirit whom God has given to those who obey Him." **verse 32**. I longed to do the right thing obey please Jesus I gazed at the way they killed on a Cross, "Hung Him High Stretched Him Wide for me He Died," a taste of a song writer penned for such a time, so "we ought to obey God rather than men" written above.

Even so, inner outward struggles attacked my mind. Emptiness crept in and crushed my spirit; made me think I wasn't good enough for God to use and express myself. For, I am nothing, yet by the grace of God it wasn't about me, my help comes from Him that breathed my assignment in my spirit. I got my answer. A song writer's hit record titled, "All to Jesus I Surrender All." God knows all about everything even all investments building funds, youth funds, poor saint offerings. God is faithful; I love Him and invest in giving. It happened a certain Sunday; my new pastor opened the doors of the church. He invited anyone to come to the altar to accept Jesus or for prayer, I went for prayer. A young lady asked my name I told her; my pastor heard her; he said that he wondered who I was, since my tithe-offering was always on time. He said I was "present in spirit," absent in the flesh. Even so I wasn't exempt from struggles in or out of the building.

A thought leaped in my spirit, he is a wise man absolutely it's the Word. "GOD IS A Spirit. And they that worship Him must worship in spirit and truth." **John 4:24**. But the word leaked that I was a backslider. As a witness for God, I make my case abundantly even if I had backslidden His invitation says. "Return, O backsliding children, says the LORD; for I AM married to you, I will take you one from a city and two from a family and I will bring you to Zion. And I will give you shepherds according to My heart, who will feed you with knowledge and understanding." **Jeremiah 3:14-15.** Delightedly God said "Then it shall come to pass, when you are multiplied and increased in the land in those days, that they will say no more. The ark of the covenant of the LORD. It shall not come to mind, nor shall they remember it, nor shall they visit it, nor shall it be made anymore." **verse 16**. A thought in mind its' no fake words watch God and believe Him.

"At that time Jerusalem shall be called: The throne of the LORD, and all the nations shall be gathered to it, to the name of the LORD, to Jerusalem. No more shall they follow the dictates of their evil hearts." **Verse 17 see 18-21.** "Return, you backsliding-children, I will heal your backsliding. Indeed, we do come to you, for You are the LORD our God. Indeed, we come to you. For You are the LORD our God." **Verses 22-23**. God is a heart Man absolutely, for He know everyone by name see **verses 24-25** a must read out loud at anyone. The group, black lives matter I believe my hope, and prayer is that killing stop for all people, especially black on black crimes. The power of God, Ruler, Creator, LORD our King in heaven, on earth and all things; east, west, north south and all in between, continues He is LORD.

Moreover, a young black boy twelve-year-old, a six grader was shot to death in the, streets of our hometown West Memphis, Arkansas by a policeman. I wept much, for it could have been one of my grandsons being a heavy burden I wrote a taste in my first book and 2nd edition; someone called a meeting I attended it. A huge concerned crowd was present the young man, mom, cried abundantly, so a concerned pastor set up another meeting. I attended, as did pastors, preachers, citizens, both men, and women came together to pray to comfort and help the family. I invited other members of our church, who could meet with us, others church members. Moreover, the group set up a fund and each one of us donated a taste of cash in case we had to help them.

And, or in case we had to travel with the family, we met faithfully once a week in a church in West Memphis. I believe had we continued meeting in a group we may have been organized to minister young men, black lives matter. I invited some members in the church I attend to come pray for the family, and, said to a member if ever Rev Al Sharpton an expert over National Action net-work planned to come to our hometown it was time. While I thought on these things the mother of the child had invited him to come eulogized her son. How great is our God? He's infinite; no limits, amazing charge to keep even in struggles, church doors opened.

The concerned group, moved forward; met at city hall with our mayor, a huge group filled the place to testify in behalf of the family. I quoted the sons of Korah revelation says. "Mercy and truth have met together: Righteousness and peace have kissed. Truth shall spring out of the earth. And righteousness shall look down from heaven. Yes, the LORD will give what is good; the land will increase. Righteousness shall go before Him. And shall make His footstep our pathway." **Psalm 85:10-12**. The mayor, who helped me at age of 21, being in a personal struggle, I asked him for an extension on my light bill, he refused said if he helped me at that time I would always be in line asking for help. I worked daily, and did not apply for welfare. He was head man at West Memphis Utilities. How Great is our God? Amazing places, even in struggles? I made it.

More abundantly, my lights remained on, the God of heaven and earth is LORD. A woman present, in the place heard me, and, said out loud she isn't lying, she asked for an extension was denied also. The court-room was packed others testified in behalf of the family's loss, terrible things concerned white leaders kept hidden; howbeit none of us can hide from our invisible God. The group traveled to the state building in Little Rock, AR. Men and women showed compassion to the family huge crowds gathered prayed fervently helped the family to endure best we could. An Action Net worker asked me to humanize the deceased young man in Little Rock, for it could've been one of my grandsons. A bitter sweet pleasure our great God of heaven blessed me, I opened my mouth to speak influence by the Spirit abundant power of the LORD was present.

The principal of the elementary school, the 6th grader attended, said he was a very good student and didn't bother anyone, the two of us, members of the same church. I pass on, a case is on record for anyone to see. I move on black lives matter to Him. So, I remember from whence we came from God keeps us praying; good principles work to advise young men God approves good morals to act on. Being faithful and true to Him, the concerned group met faithfully from the year of July 2007 to 2009; points to the hall of fame, redeeming the time God's glory is Jesus Christ the good Servant teach good principles truly. Therefore, amazing places even in struggles show summation of my first chapter Paul declared, "For though I am absent in the flesh, yet I am with you in the spirit, rejoicing to see your good order and steadfastness of your faith In Christ." **Colossians 2:5.** Get set, a charge to keep even in struggles. More abundantly our mission circle planned a Christmas feast at my house a week before time.

I asked my granddaughter to lead a song, with help from her little sister and brother she agreed. They sang a song amazingly I believe entitled, "I Don't Know What You Come to do, but I came To Praise the LORD, I Didn't Come to look at you." They sounded like experts trained them before our feast began. One of our mission members said it was the first time she attended a mission feast, kids sang for elders like my grands. The kids made a joyful noise to the LORD; as a result, two of my grandsons play instruments in Junior high bands. I wished they could've been in place to make a joyful noise with their instruments at the feast a week or so before Christmas.

Even so, my younger grandson entered a state contest in Little Rock Arkansas for junior high and he was elected to participate in it; a hall of fame wonderful blessing to us. Also, my younger granddaughter at age four memorized Bibles verses I taught her; **John 3:16, Genesis 1:1**, and **Proverbs 22:6**; she passed on to her sister, and brothers. As results I thank God weekly Bible study paid off in my house. Even so, at age seventeen inner out struggles causes to her to err big time yet His Word is a sure thing. So, God saved a wretch like me; she loved to open devotion before Bible study with prayer and a praise song, the enemy is out to win. Joel the prophet of Judah, the southern kingdom and His people everywhere passed on says: "Tell your children about it. Let your children tell their children. And their children another generation." **Joel 1:3**.

My hope is that young millennials petition God themselves, and practice daily to please Him. During the days of Joshua, a new generation entered Canaan see **Joshua 1:1-7**. "This Book of the Law shall not depart from your mouth but you should meditate in it day and night that you may observe to do according to all that is written in it. Then you will make your way prosperous, then you will have good success." **Verse 8**. So, verse 9 hang on my south bedroom wall for moral support with immense principles questions. "Have I not commanded you? Be strong and of good courage, do not be dismayed, for the LORD your God is with you wherever you go." God used Joshua to write most of the book, I believe by faith in Him, be of 'good courage.'

Moreover, I make mention of the black farmers, heirs co-heirs and attempted farmers, the word was out the year 1918. A woman, a black farmer applied for black farmers money failed to receive it. My hope is that her heirs receive their reward every dollar. I wrote in my first book and 2nd edition titled above, since Paul wrote. "For you have not received the spirit of bondage again to fear; but you have received the Spirit of adoption whereby we cry Abby Father. The Spirit Himself bears witness with our spirit that we are the children of God then—heirs; heirs of God and joint-heirs with Christ; if so be that we suffer with

Him, that we be also gloried together." **Romans 8:15-17**. An heir is one who has lawfully right to receive a title or property of an older member of the family who in dies. In that God sent His Son to redeem those who were under the law. Repeatedly it is in this book, God has made us heirs of salvation read the Word.

CHAPTER TWO

"A CHARGE TO KEEP EVEN IN STRUGGLES"

I make my request to God, who said to me write the book. I asked Him six words: 'Where do I go from here?' He dropped two words in my spirit, one is: Expedient means, useful effecting a desired result, suited to circumstance convenient and two is: Expedite means to speed up, make easy, quick. God quicken my spirit expedited words from above He knows my circumstances. Even in times of inner outer struggles, the greatness of salvation is to trust and believe God answers our request expediently. After Paul's greetings, he wrote. "We give thanks to God always for you all, making mention of you in our prayers, remembering without ceasing your work of faith, labor of love and patience of hope in our LORD Jesus Christ in the sight of our God and Father." **I Thessalonians 1:2-3**. So, I thank our God going forth to pen these things.

Paul preached great examples to us: "Knowing, beloved brethren, Your election by God. For our gospel did not come to you in word only, but also in power, and in the Holy Spirit and in much assurance, as you know what kind of men we were among for your sake. And you became followers of us and of the LORD, having received the Word in much affliction, with joy of the Holy Spirit." **Verses 4-6**. So, whether inner outer struggles, in affliction sorrow or pain my belief is God is always available to us my desire is be an example likewise; Paul got it passed on said. "So that you became examples to all Macedonia and Achaia, who believe. For from you the Word of the LORD has sounded forth, not only Macedonia and Achaia, but also in every place. Your faith toward God has gone out, so that we do not need to say anything." **Verses 7-8**.

Paul preached my absolute true story concern my God given faith, my labor of love, patience, and hope I declare isn't easy, yet He is faithful says. "For they themselves declare concerning us what matter of entry we had for you, and how you turned to God from idols to serve the living and true God, and wait for His son from heaven, whom He raised from the dead, even Jesus who delivers us from the wrath to come." **Verses 9-10**. Remarkably, Paul had a vision from God. "A man from Macedonia stood and pleaded with him, saying: Come over to Macedonia and help us. Now he had seen the vision, immediately we sought to go to Macedonia, concluding that the LORD had called us to preach the gospel to them." **Acts 16:9b-10**. The lesson is remarkably greater than great, for, I had a vision from God in this same chapter **Acts 16**. My third chapter titled, A time to shout even in struggles. God is my witness my invitation is on record so be it.

"And Moses hid his face from God, for he was afraid to look upon God." **Exodus 3:6b**. God said while studying my Bible the year 2009, I was set to return to church, He said. "You shall not go empty-handed." Incredible overwhelmed I opened my Bible found the words. **Exodus 3:21b**. I reread the entire verse, "And I will give this people favor in the sight of the Egyptians: when you go you shall not go empty-handed I believed Him. God spoke a radio station in my spirit; equipment to operate it, trained in journalism to teach with pay, edits books, etc. God's divine spoken revelation was more than I can transcribe even now, yet I believe Him. Mindfully aware, Moses did not understand a miracle the bush burned, yet, "The angel of the LORD" did. "The bush was burning with fire, but the bush was not consumed." **Exodus 3:2b**.

I researched my Bible miraculously. **Exodus 23:15b** says, "And none shall appear before me empty-handed." I reread the chapter shared it one time not a word was uttered. Whether spoken or notable in His Word, many great things happened redeeming the time for me meant. "He must increase, but I must decrease." **John 3:30**. So it happened. I believe God ordained a family of missionaries, husband, wife, and their two siblings sent them abroad to foreign nations. To teach the Gospel of Jesus Christ as did many Paul and others some churches in our hometown, helped supported their miraculous works of God by the Spirit. The missionary family returned to the states held a workshop she learned abroad remarkably the way people lived in other nations.

Years later, I walked into a Christian book store and noticed a book titled *The Pursuit of Excellence*. I purchased and read it. The author taught remarkably ways to pursue great things. A taste of the story revealed an eagle, I believe, didn't know it could fly. The bird stayed in the pen with chicken so long it thought it was a chicken. Its' been a long time since I read the book, but one day the eagle found out it could fly. So the eagle lifted its' powerful wings in the beautiful blue skies created birds to fly. Jesus said, "Look at the birds of the air, for they neither sow or reap nor gather into barns: yet your heavenly Father feeds them. Are you not of more value than they?" **Matthew 6:26.** I considered with deep regret someone borrowed my book and failed to return it. A song a writer penned I enjoy I believe, entitled "I Believe I can fly."

So, a member of the church we serve informed us Sunday, September 13, 2015 that she received an email from the missionary, I believe, ordained by God to carry the Gospel to Africa and foreign nations. She said the family returned to their hometown, she became ill. I asked for a copy of her email and knew the missionaries also. Her email said, "You may remember when we served in Mozambique we asked you to pray for a Radio Station which reaches into Mwangi villages. You prayed the LORD answered with Normand and Henrietta, they will be going on their scheduled Home assignment the end of the year. With deep regret if no one is found to replace them. Aim will need to close the Radio Station. Nuri, maybe that someone is you! Amazing places even in struggles, I felt like shouting because it looked like one of God's miracles.

From 'the burning bush' that was not consumed I was humbled to the core of my heart and soul as results. The email explained my vision, the year of 2009, God dropped in my spirit a Radio Station etc. I dated in my Bible the same year above; **see Exodus 34:20b**. Also see Deuteronomy **16:16b,** "And they shall not appear before the LORD empty-handed titled: The Passover reviewed mindful that Ruth left the foreign nation of Moab to be with her mother-in-law Naomi, she didn't return 'empty-handed;' anonymously a writer wrote the book **Ruth 3:17b**. Mindful of His immeasurable miracles God works; acts and wonders more abundantly, is from my heart.

So, a miracle happened a group of activists marched celebrated Memorial Day in memory of Rev. Martin Luther King in Memphis TN. My daughter and I marched with the group. A Disc Jockey was among the activists, he was very kind a witness for Christ. A thought leaped in my mind again a "burning bush not consume' miracle. To meet a D.J. face to face in a Hugh crowd of people, a supernatural blessing. I asked the D.J. the cost of supplies to operate a Radio Station he didn't hesitate quoted miracle prices at that time, my hope a sure thing even today. How could I know the missionary became ill returned to her hometown or penned an E-mail concerned a Radio Station that I cannot forget it, or, how would I meet a D. J. a witness for God? So, I wait on God and in hope of fruition a very great miracle day in memory of the Rev. Martin Luther King, a witness for life in Jesus Christ, who is the glory forevermore.

The missionary wanted to go shopping. My friend was alive during those days. So, the two of us were delighted to take her. She had own money to shop with in the great city of Memphis TN. also, great to be in good company being on her mailing list; we moved for the betterment of God's blessings to us. Years later my dear friend passed away God rest her soul. At time emptiness struggled to enter my mind the Word of God and my given senses to know good, versus, evil especially before every great blessing yet let hope, faith, work, trust Him. The missionary will get a copy of my book. Solomon passed to generations good moral principles to all. "My son, do not forget my law. But let your heart keep my commands: for length of days and long life and peace they will add to you. Let not mercy and truth forsake you: Bind them around your neck. Write them on the table of your heart. And find favor and high esteem in the sight of God and man." **Proverbs 3:1-4**. Manifest His good life, the cream of the crop is planted in Him, by Him, and through Him, the glory the power and Spirit I practice daily to; "Trust in the LORD with all your heart: lean not to your own understanding: In all your ways acknowledge Him, and He shall direct your path. Do not be wise in your own eyes. Fear the LORD and depart from evil. It will be health to your flesh. And strength to your bones. Honor the LORD with your possessions. And with the first fruits of all your increase." **Verses 5-9**.

God is our Provider. "So, your barns will be filled with plenty, and your vats will overflow with new wine.

My son, do not despise the chastening of the LORD, nor detest His correction. For whom the LORD loves He corrects, just as a father in whom he delights. Happy is the man that finds wisdom, and understanding who gains knowledge;" **Proverbs 3:10-13**. I believe the blessing in strange blessings by His good pleasures dreams visions understanding by faith in God. Solomon says, "Surely, He scorns the scornful, but give grace to the humble. The wise shall inherit glory. But shame shall be the legacy of fools." **Proverbs 3:34-35.** So, I see two-way breathtaking paths sincere in Him; I use when I don't know where to turn, or, the way to escape emptiness God helps us to overcome inner outer struggles according the God of heaven in us on earth.

I notated in my book and second edition titled above God said the year of 2010 Obamacare, the (A.C.A.) The Affordable Care Act will prosper, I believe God and last Words last page. **See Psalm 72:5-7**. Hopefully will come to fruition, "For with God nothing is impossible." **Luke 1:37**. I wait, watch and pray my God given faith works. The Obamas helped Hillary to run for president. She promised a plan better for all Americans better healthcare. A charge to keep even in struggles the Word is; "He shall have dominion also from sea to sea and from the River to the ends of the earth. They that dwell in the wilderness will bow before Him, and His enemies shall lick the dust. The kings of Tarshish, the isles shall bring presents: and Sheba shall offer gifts. Yea, all the kings shall fall down before Him: all nations shall serve Him." **Psalm 72: 8-11:**

So, it happened; "He shall deliver the needy when he cries; the poor also, and him that has no helper. He shall spare the poor and the needy. He shall redeem Their soul from deceit and violence; and precious shall be in His sight." **Verses 12-14**. See dominion power **Genesis 1:26**.

Solomon said, "And He shall live; the gold of Sheba will be given to Him, Prayer will be made for Him continually, and daily He shall be praised. There will be an abundance of grain in the earth, on the top of the mountains; its fruit shall wave like Lebanon; and those of the children shall flourish like grass of the earth." **Verses 15-16**. To flourish is to bloom, and prosper, God is Omniscient all-knowing, Solomon says. "His name shall endure forever; His name shall continue as the sun. And men shall call Him blessed in Him. All nations shall call Him blessed. Blessed me "And blessed be His glorious name forever: and let the whole earth be filled with His glory: Amen, and Amen. The prayers of David ended." Psalm 72:**19-20,** the end of the glory story.

      The name Eliphaz means (my God is dispenser) the leader of Job's three friend he asked Job "Should a wise man answer with empty knowledge, and fill himself with the east wind? Should he reason with unprofitable talk, or by speeches with which he can do no good? Yes, you can cast off fear, and restrain prayer before God. For your iniquity teaches your mouth, and you choose the tongue of the crafty." **Job 15:2-5**. Eliphaz, repeated no new thing to Job. But he accused him says "Your mouth condemns you, and not I: Yes, your own lips testify against you. Are you the first man who was born? Were you made before the hills? Have you heard the counsel of God? Do you limit wisdom to yourself? What do you know that we do not know?" **Verses 6-9a, see 9b-35.**

      Job's friend discussed eight notable questions I believe asked, "Can a man be profitable to God. Though he who is wise may be profitable to himself? Is it any pleasure to the Almighty that you are righteous? Or is it any gain to Him that you make your ways blameless? Is it because of your fear of Him that He corrects you? And enters judgment with you? For you have taken pledges from your brother for no reason, and stripped the naked of their clothing." **Job 22:2-6**. My genuine beliefs are profitable, the Almighty made a way for me to escape emptiness more than I know a friend of Job asked. "Is not God in the height of heaven? And behold the height of the stars, how high they are. And you say, what does God know? Can He judge through deep darkness? Thick clouds cover Him, so that He cannot see. And He walks above the circle of heaven. Will you keep the old way, which wicked men trod who were cut down before their time, whose foundations were swept away by a flood?" **Job 22.10-16**.

Jesus used a parable to teach religious leaders simple lessons who challenged Him for certain reasons genuinely God made the height of heaven, the earth, seas and the wind. "Then He began to tell the parable: A certain man planted a vineyard, leased it to vain dresses and went into a far country for a long time. Now at vintage-time he sent a servant to the husbandmen, that they should give him some of the fruit of the vineyard: but the husbandmen beat him, and sent him away empty-handed." **Luke 20:9-10**. The servant returned with nothing. "Again, he sent another servant: and they beat him also, and entreated him shamefully, and sent him away empty handed. And again, he sent a third: they wounded him and cast him out." **Verses 11-12**.

Amazing places even in struggles. "Then said the owner of the vineyard said: What shall I do? I will send my beloved son: probably they will respect him when they see him. But when the vine-dressers saw him, they reasoned among themselves, said this is the heir. Come, let us kill him, that the inheritance may be ours so, they cast him out killed him, therefore, what will the owner of the vineyard do to them? **Verses 13-15**. Seem like Jesus parable didn't mean nothing to them says. "He will come and destroy those vinedressers and give the vineyard to others. And when they heard it they said, certainly not! Then He looked at them and said, what is this that is written. The stone which the builders rejected Has become the chief cornerstone. Whosoever falls on that stone will be broken; but whom it falls on, it will grind him to power."

Then the evidence reminds me of God's beloved Son: "And the chief priest and the scribes that very hour sought to lay hands on Him, but they feared the people, for they knew He had spoken the parable against them." **Verse 19**. My dear readers what do you think? Jesus Parables illustrates or demonstrates experts' chief priests, scribes rejected Jesus, emptiness even in high places says. "So, they watched Him, and sent spies who pretended to be righteous, that they might seize on His words, in other to deliver Him to the power and authority of the governor. Then they asked Him, saying: Teacher, we know that You say and teach rightly, and you do not show personal favoritism, but teach the way of God in truth: Is it lawful for us to pay taxes to Caesar or not?" **verses 19-22**. A charge to keep even in struggles. They couldn't fool Jesus, nor can anyone, experts' not even spies pretending they feared the people. **See verses 23-26.** A charge to keep even in struggles. For example, a young man was sent to work on fixtures in my home.

So, it happened we greeted, exchanged name chatted a few minutes about life in general. He said he loved God, his wife and two children enjoyed the work he did. He was excited; the Affordable Care Act dropped two-hundred dollars per month that year. I informed him if young people invest in the plan it will cost less; the plan will flourished also insure, dental and optical care. I recall, a king whose charge to keep went wrong in amazing struggles, as reminders to me. An elderly lady always said; God sits high and looks low. A song writer penned titled I believe. "His eyes are on the spirals, I know He watches over me." But do you believe? "The eyes of the LORD are in every place. Keeping watch on the evil and the good. **Proverbs 15:3**. The A.C.A. Act isn't fake news. The question is who you believe my dear reader. Who is king of the fake news?

"Once upon a time" it happened, "All this came upon Nebuchadnezzar. At the end of 12 months he came walking about the royal palace of Babylon. The king spoke, saying: Is not this great Babylon, that I have built for a royal dwelling by my mighty power and for the honor of my majesty?" **Daniel 4:28-30**. To make it plain I refer to the Word of God says. "While the word was still in the king's mouth, a voice fell from heaven: king Nebuchadnezzar, to you it is spoken the kingdom has departed from you!" **Verse 31**. The king didn't earn majesty at all; his Struggles continued it happened for the world to know the king wasn't too big to fail we reap and sow

My hope is that leaders know these things the truth so it happened saying. "And they shall drive you from men, and your dwelling place shall make you eat grass like oxen: and seven times shall pass over you, until you know that the Most-High rules in the kingdom of men, and gives it to whosoever He chooses." **Verse 32**. So it happened. "That hour the Word was fulfilled concerned Nebuchadnezzar; he was driven from men and ate grass like oxen: his body was wet with the dew of heaven till his hair had grown like eagles' feathers and his nails like birds." **Verse 33**.

God test His people, leaders are not exempted. Nebuchadnezzar was tested abundantly he said. "And at the end of the time I, Nebuchadnezzar, lifted my eyes to heaven, and my understanding returned to me; and I blessed the Most-High and praised and honored Him who lives forever. For His dominion is an everlasting dominion, and His kingdom is from generation to generation." **Daniel 4:34**. The king understood in the fullness of God's timing He is LORD testified: "All the inhabitants of the earth are reputed as nothing; He does according to His will in the army of heaven and among the inhabitants of the earth. No one can refrain His hand. Or say to Him, what have you done?" **Verses 35**. The king talked like a born-again man of God. So, the king's testified did he not know one reaps what he sows even leaders? Nebuchadnezzar declared.

"At the same time, my reason returned to me, and for the glory of my kingdom, my honor and splendor returned to me. My counselors and nobles resorted to me, I was restored to my kingdom and excellent majesty was added to me." **verse 36**. The king acted like, I believe, thought he earned God's glory but found out the purified truth says. "Now I, Nebuchadnezzar, praise and extol and honor the King of heaven, all whose works are true, and His ways justice. And those who walk in pride He can put to death." **Verse 37**. The king got it, the dreams should have cause him to refer to he said "Look! He answered. I see four men loose, walking during the fire; and they are not hurt, and the form of the fourth is like the Son of God." **Daniel 3:25**. Like, "the bush was burning with fire, but the bush was not consumed." **Exodus 3:3b**.

God knows the way to get our attention, during David's generation, he said. "O LORD my God, in You I put my trust; save me from all those who persecute me: and deliver me, lest they tear me like a lion, rending me to pieces, while there is none to deliver. O LORD my God, if I have done this if there is iniquity in my hands." **Psalm**

7:1-3. "Sweet psalmist of Israel," said, "If I have repaid evil to him who was at peace with me. Or have plundered my enemy without cause pursue me and overtake me yes, let him trample my life to the earth. And lay my honor to the dust." **Verses 4-5**. He examined his heart in many powerful struggles emptiness attacked his spirit said. "Arise, O Lord in Your angry; Lift yourself up because of the rage of my enemies: Rise up for me to judgment You have commanded! So, the congregation of the people surround You: For their sakes, therefore, return on high. The LORD shall judge the people." **Verses 6-8**.

David's charge points the people to surround God, he confessed. "For the righteous God test the hearts and minds." Verse 9b. Moving forward David added: "He made a pit and dug it, and has fallen into the ditch which he made. His trouble shall return upon his own head, and his violent dealing shall come down on his own crown. I will praise the LORD accordingly, to His righteousness. And will sing praise to the name of the LORD Most High." **Psalm 7:15-17**. Can you dig these things? So, I considered a dream like I stepped in a puddle of quick sand, my feet got stuck in the wet sand, I was very scared no one around to pull me out. I cried out to God in my dream to help me abruptly He woke me up safe. I blessed our God of Heaven, earth and the seas yes, I can dig it! I observe our God our team of witnesses whether right or wrong.

So, the team passed out tracks in the streets of our hometown, two question marks ?? Show on the outside, the track asked, "Do you know?" the opened tract asked, "Do you know for sure that you are going to be with God in Heaven?" Some listeners said no one knows who's going to heaven, wait, there is good news, apostle John wrote **I John 5:13-21**. I copied the Word above in my first chapter, it is a choice, heaven or hell. Reminiscing, on the Word of

God Nicodemus, one of few religious leaders believed Him. "And Nicodemus, who at first came to Jesus at night, also came, bringing a mixture of myth and aloes about a hundred pounds." **John 19:39**. It is said, "They took the body of Jesus, and bound it in strips of linen and spices, as the custom of the Jews is to bury. Now in the place where He was crucified there was a garden, and in the garden, was a new tome, in which no one had laid. So, they laid Jesus, because of the Jews Preparation Day, for the tome was nearby." **John 19:40-42.**

My God breathe assignment gives me great pleasure, straight to evidence says "Then they said to them, why do you seek the living among the dead? He is not here but is risen! **Luke 24:5b**. Mindfully aware, after our grandparents passed away, I invested in the evidence to follow the money; twenty-year paid life insurance policies, for four siblings. The insurance agents were door to door salesmen, at that time, the company closed its' doors. Today as a senior citizen it's not my imagination, to the core of my soul God, sits high looks low, another loss no one can trace and seek these things out. It is another journey, for example to learned about farmers inheritances and their heirs tried to follow our money yet we continue to wait. Even so, monies taken out of our paychecks by East Central Agency, experts, their lawyers said for three years; was withheld, but not paid into Social Security. So, the agency didn't pay staff personal vacation pay, up to two-hundred forty hour, mindful I'm just saying it is not my or our imagination.

I'm one that says don't mess with my earned Medicare, my personal investment. Imagine, if seniors were rewarded all the money due them today, cash money would flow throughout America paid in full; Black farmer's heirs of the promise. What a prosperous journey it could be! It is written, The New Unger's Bible Dictionary page 921; Nicodemus was the third richest man of Jerusalem. But it is said his daughter was seen gathering barley corn for food under, horses' feet. Some have conjectured the result of the persecutions he received having embraced Christianity **John 3:1**. The rich man didn't quit or give up; he had to meet Jesus I believe it was a divine God breathed assignment planned before his birth to invest in Him.

I promised the staff, that remain alive in Him, I will make mention in every book God approves for me to write that we worked tirelessly at East Central Arkansas Agency many years. I was elated one of my former staff persons called, to wish me a happy birthday. She was saddled down with inner outer struggles, disabled to work she found out a monthly disability check was too small to live on. So, she continues to work disabled. Imagine again the agency's lawyer revealed to us on July 03, 2013 the last time we met with a judge: (a sixteen year' class action lawsuit failed.) He met with us; said our case was not filed in court. How awesome are inner outer struggles? A charge to keep even in struggles; the staff even met with our lawyers, and a judge who promised we would get paid, the judge a deacon of a church in Cross County one we served elders in his hometown knew our true story. But he left town to judge other places God is great He approves women today to work together petitioning the high places to help others. An anonymous psalmist, reveal absolute confidence from our Most High God says.

"The LORD builds up Jerusalem; He gathers together the outcasts of Israel. He heals the brokenhearted and binds up their wounds. He counts the number of stars; He calls them by name. Great is our LORD, and mighty in power; His understanding is infinite. The LORD lifts up the humble; He casts the wicked down to the ground." **Psalm 147:2-6**. The words manifest genuine love in my heart; even a charge to keep in struggles; revisit **verses 7-17**. So, the writer says, "He sends out His Word and melts them; He cause the wind to blow, and the waters flow. He declares His Word to Jacob." **Verses 18-19**. I've learned to share the Word in marketplaces; His awesome blessings continue. A member of the same church we attend said God revealed to her Obama would be 44th president of the United States and her, children were witnesses we rejoiced together elated with the joy of God. The sky sun, moon etc. above are handy works of God.

Paul made the case says. "And we know that all things work together for good to those who Love God, to those who are called according, to His propose," Romans 8:28. Believers know for sure obedience glories God, "For who He foreknew, He also predestined to be conformed to the image of His Son, that He might be the firstborn among many. Moreover, whom He predestined, these He also called; Whom He called, these He also justified; who He justified these He also glorified." **8:29-30**. God's words cling like my own skin; cover my flesh and bones, Paul asked, "What then shall we say to these things? If God is for us, who can be against us?" **Verse 31**. The answer is no one, like a record recorded in my mind past, present even future blessings Paul asked three questions and answered says. "He who did not spare His Own Son, but delivered Him up for us all, how shall He not freely give us all things? Who shall bring a charge against God's own elect? It is God who justifies." **Verses 32-33**. Love continue in Him.

Clothed in the mind of Christ; covered by the blood of Jesus God gave up His Only Son saying. "Who is he who condemns? It is Christ who died, and furthermore is also risen, who is even at the right hand of God, who also makes intercession for us. Who shall separate us from the love of Christ? Shall tribulation, or distress, or persecution, or famine, or nakedness, or peril, or sword? As it is written." **34-35**. All things work breath of life come from God, my health, my hope: "It is written: for Your sake, we are killed all day long: We are accounted as sheep for the slaughter. Yet in all these we are more than conquerors through Him who loved us. For I am persuaded that neither depth, nor any other created thing, shall be able to separate us from the love of God in Christ Jesus our LORD." **Verses 36-39**. A Mighty Jesus Is He who saves us.

   I walked to the bus stop on a day that was extremely cold, I waited on the bus to go to work in Memphis. It was freezing cold that wintery day even the bus driver didn't show up for work. So, I made my case to God had no feeling in my feet: I said LORD, if you allow me to return home safely I will stay home in freezing weather so, I returned safe by grace. Aware of struggles I crawl on the floor at times today in respect to God by faith bowed to Him as did this woman. "Having a flow of blood for twelve years, who spent all her money and could not be healed she came from behind and touched the border of His garment and immediately her flow of blood stopped." **Luke 8:43-44**. The woman's name is not on record, unknown to us only Jesus knows just right for "Jesus said: Who touched Me?" **Verse 45**. I wonder who? **See verses 46-48**.

   David said. "Bow down Your ear, O LORD hear me: for I am poor and needy: Preserve my soul; for I am holy; O my God save your servant that trust in You. Be merciful to me LORD; for I cry to You daily." **Psalm 86:1-3**. Rich and poor a charge was made says, "All nations whom You have made shall come and worship before You, O LORD; and shall glorify Your name. For You are great and do wondrous things: You alone are God." **Verses 9-10**. So, David said, "Teach me Your way, O LORD, I will walk in Your truth; Unite my heart to fear Your name. I will praise You O LORD with all my heart, to fear Your name forevermore. For great is Your mercy toward me; and You have delivered my soul from the lowest hell. O God, the proud have risen against me, and a mob of violent men sought my life, and have not set You before them." **Verses 11-14**.

What if men today react to God's teaching as did David? Even when the mob was against David, he blessed God and it worked he said. "But You O LORD, are full of compassion, and gracious, longsuffering and abundant in mercy and truth." **verse 15**. David prayed and said, "Give Your strength to Your servant and save the son, of Your maidservant. Show me a sign for good, that those who hate me may see it and be ashamed: Because You, LORD, have helped and comforted me." **Verse 16-17**. God knows we are weak, but we can depend on Him. A charge to keep even in struggles, a song writer penned "I have to cry sometimes," and yet I trust Him whole-heartily, it works as results, I ask God to wrap us up in His love grace mercy and truth abundantly.

Psalm teaches us incredible ways to survive in good and hard times. For example, my friend's dog took sick. They loved it as a family member. I repeated an old saying leaped in my spirit says. "A hound dog licks its master's hand and worship him, a man's best friend." They took their dog to the vet it refused to eat, the doctor examined their dog it had leukemia an infection in the blood. The vet suggested they put the dog to sleep, they rejected the vet's advice. As friends from our former school, 'Wonder' a few days past he called again with glee in his voice said their pet was eating that was good feed-back to the entire family.

So, he called me a week later inner outer struggles began, pain, hurt and sorrow was in his voice, he said his loving wife of fifty-one years passed away suddenly. I was speechless and sensed his incredible pain at the loss of his loving faithful wife. I considered David's words struggled to survive he trusted God said.

"My God, My God, why have You forsaken Me? Why are You so far from helping Me. And from the words of My groaning? O My God, I cry in the daytime. But You do not hear: and in the night season, and am not silent. But You are holy. Enthroned in the praises of Israel. Our fathers trusted in you: They trusted and You delivered them." **Psalm 22:1-4** Months of fervent constant prayer on our phones my friend said his beloved wife of fifty-one years wasn't coming back. He said their only granddaughter kept on crying, the dog barked searched for her in every room. And he felt guilty because she had a fatal heart attack; and didn't suffer at all, he was the one who suffered with heart problems for many years and cried out to God to heal him.

David responded said:" They cried to You, and were delivered; they trusted in You, and were "delivered. They trusted in You and were not ashamed." **Verse 5**. I could have imagined my friend's incredible pain, because my beloved husband passed away, disabled for years. My friend probable felt like David this psalm, a prayer points to great suffering also incredible joy. "For the kingdom is the LORD." **Psalm 22:28**. God s rules over our health, sufferings life and death. Glimpses, show Deborah, a woman Judge all Israel God called her name to work a wise woman counselor, an expert in all of her duties and moral principles because she trusted God to use her.

"Then, Deborah and Barak the son of Abinoam sang on that day, saying: When leaders lead in Israel, when the people willingly offer themselves. Bless the LORD. Hear O kings: Give ear O princes! I, even, I will sing praises to the LORD; I will sing praises to the LORD of Israel." **Judges 5:1**. So, "They chose new gods; then there was war in the gates: Not a shield or spear was seen among forty thousand in Israel. My heart is with the rulers of Israel who offered themselves willingly with the people. Bless the LORD!" **Verses 8-9; see 10-30.** Fast forward says. "So, let all your enemies perish O LORD; but let those who love Him be like the sun when it comes out in full strength. The land had rest for forty years." **Judges 5:31**.

Gideon, had conspicuous struggles: see **Judges Chapters 6-8.** He had a charge to keep even in struggles. "Then LORD turned to him and said," Go in this might of yours, and you shall save Israel from the hand of the Midianites. Have I not sent you? So, he said to Him: Oh, my LORD, how can I save Israel? Behold my family is poor in Manasseh, and I am the least in my father's house." **Judges 6:14-15**. After Sunday school ends, all classes come together, our superintendent asked did anyone find their name in the lesson. I said yes. Gideon's excuses sound like my own. God said write the book, He did it for my own good conspicuously exceedingly a shield of faith David's record say. "But You O LORD, are a shield for me, my glory and the One who lifts up my head. I cried to the LORD with my voice. And He heard me from His holy hill, I lay down and slept: I awoke, for the LORD sustained me, I will not be afraid of ten-thousands of people who set themselves against me. **Psalm 3:3-6.**

By faith, it is written the way to escape these things David grabbed hold of it says. "Arise, O LORD, save me, O my God!" **Verse 7a**. Because by faith in God is our shield the evidence says. "Salvation belongs to the LORD. Your blessing is upon Your people." **Verse 8**. I observe the birth of Moses, Exodus chapter two, but first chapter reveals slavery the people suffered inner outer struggles in Egypt. Moses story is greater than awesome. "By faith he was hidden three months by his parents, because they saw he was a beautiful child: they were not afraid of the king's command. By faith Moses, when he became of age refused to be called the son of Pharaoh's daughter. Choosing rather to suffer affliction with the people of God than to enjoy the pleasures of sin" **Hebrews 11:23-25**.

Observe a greater charge by faith in God, "Esteeming the reproach of Christ greater riches than the treasures in Egypt, for he looked to the reward. So, it was Moses. "By faith he forsook Egypt, not fearing the wrath of the king, for he endured as seeing Him who is invisible. By faith kept the Passover and the sprinkling of blood, lest he who destroyed the firstborn should touch them. By faith they passed through the Red Sea as the dry land, whereas the Egyptians, attempting to do so, were drown." **verses 27-29**.

Even so, the hall of faith chapter calls many people by name says. "For the time, would fail me to tell me of Gideon, of Barak, and of Samson, and Jephthah; of David, and the prophets. Through faith subdued kingdoms wrought righteousness obtained promises stopped the mouths of lions; Escaped the edge of the sword, in God having provided better things for us." **39-40**.

Gideon had a limited vision, he had doubts felt inadequate God called his name he obeyed Him Barak said to Deborah "if you go I will go" a taste of 4:8. Samson, dedicated to God from birth as a Nazirite. "Jephthah said to them: My people and I were in a great struggle with the people of Ammon. And when I called, you did not deliver me, I took my life in my own hands and crossed over against the people of Ammon; and the LORD delivered them into my hand. Why have you come up to me this day to fight against me?" **Judges 12:2-4**. David, the greatest king of Israel. Ancestor of Jesus Christ; God refer to him "a man after My own heart." See **Acts 13:22b**.

      Moreover, Amos, wrote to Israel the northern kingdom, people of God everywhere sayings; "But let justice run down like water, And righteousness like a mighty stream. Did you offer Me sacrifices and offerings in the wilderness forty years: O house of Israel?" **Amos 5:24-25**. Amos testified I was no prophet! See **7:14-17**. Observe these great things Paul said redeem the time of greatness; "But when the fullness of time had come, God sent forth His Son, born of a woman, born under the law. To redeem those who were under the law, that we might receive the adoption as sons. And because you are sons, God has sent forth the Spirit of His Son into your hearts, crying out. Abba, Father." **Galatians 4:4-6**. Moreover, I know inner joy come from God, the evidence approved records in many places, love, grace wisdom and truth comes from above.

      "Therefore, you are no longer a slave but a son, and if a son, then an heir of God through Christ. But now after you have known God, or rather are known by God, how is it that you turn to weak and beggarly elements, to which you desire again to be in bondage?" **Verses 7-9**. The questions remind me of our prison ministry, the ladies in bondage prayers reached heaven I believe they knew God got their attention in prison. I'm mindful of a taste the way of escape these things notable Paul added. "You observe days and months and seasons years. I am afraid for you, lest I have labored for you in vain. Brethren, I urge you to become like me, for I became like you. You have not injured me at all." **Verses 10-12**.

Paul examined himself an heir of God. "You know that because of physical infirmity I preached the gospel to you at first. And my trial which was in my flesh you did not despise or reject, but you received me as an angel of God, as Christ Jesus. What then was the blessing you enjoyed? For I bear you witness that, if possible, you would have plucked out your own eyes and given them to me. Have I therefore become your enemy because I tell you the truth?" **verses 13-16**. The truth finds us out. "They zealously court you, but for no good: yet they want to exclude, that you may be zealous for them. But it is good to be zealous in a good thing always, and not only when I am present with you. My little children, for whom I labor in birth again until Christ is formed in you. I would like to be present with you now and to change my tone: for I have doubts about you." **Verses 18-19**.

As for me, doubts cause me instant fear, a wall beautifully wall plaque shaped like a Bible hang on my north wall in my bedroom, it works by batteries. A cross encircled in **Numbers 1-12**; the word says, "ONE DAY AT A TIME." Also says, "Help me believe in what I am, show me the Stairway I have to climb LORD. For my sake, teach me to take one day at a time." The clock explains two-ways, and the Word says. "Tell me, you who desire to be under the law, do you not hear the law. For it is written Abraham had two sons, one a bondwoman, the other a free woman. But he who was born of the bondwoman was born according to the flesh. And he of the free woman of the promise, which things are symbolic." **Galatians 4: 21-24a**.

Paul made it plain for us to comprehend two-way paths inside and out even from the beginning says. "For these are the two covenants; the one from Mount Sinai which gives birth to bondage, which is Hagar. For this Hagar is in bondage with her children. But Jerusalem above is free, which is the mother of us all. For it is written: Rejoice, O barren, you who do not bear! Break forth and shout, you who are not in labor! For the desolate has many more children then she who has a husband." **Verses 24b**. A song entered my spirit "RESCUE THE PERSHING." **25**. But the Jerusalem above is free, which is the mother of us all." **Verse 26**. Glory hallelujah, the way to escape these things the song reveals Jesus rescues the perishing one-way to rejoice in Him.

      Matthew said a centurion had no doubts, "But only speak a word, and my servant will be healed." **Matthew 8:8b**. Jesus answered the centurion said, "I have not found such great faith, not even in Israel." **Verse 10b**. More abundantly it is good to know the way to escape inner outer struggles that's too hard to bear in the first place. For instance, one-night severe pain woke me up, my right arm hurt so bad like a knife grimed down deep in my arm. I prayed LORD, I can't stand this pain! About two hours passed and He healed my arm, I will always believe God knows just how much we can bear and He delivers us on right on time, the record says.

      "Now when Jesus had come into Peter's house, He saw his wife's mother lying sick with a fever. So, He touched her hand, and the fever left her. And she rose and served them. When evening had come, they brought to Him many who were demon possessed, and He cast out the spirits with a word, and He healed all that was sick." **Matthew 8:14-16**. Incredible things amazingly Jesus heals says. "That it might be fulfilled which was spoken by Isaiah the prophet saying: He Himself took our infirmities and bore our sickness." **Verse 17**. A charge to keep even in struggles. Consciously, the elders' testimonies back in the day said they could declare weather reports, warned us when dark clouds gathered in the sky it was going to rain, for they felt their pain. Likewise, when clouds gather as an elder today. I can declare the weather report because my God given conscious talks back to me even so, pain remains a part of life rain or shine "And He also said to the people: When you see, a cloud rises out of the west, immediately you say: There comes a shower: and so, it is." **Luke 12:54**. See **55-59**.

Asaph referred to God's great animal kingdom recorded. "For every beast of the forest is Mine, and the cattle of a thousand hills, I know all the birds of the mountains and the wild beast of the field are Mine." **Psalm 50:10-11**. An elder said he didn't understand a black cow gives white milk, churns to pure butter nor do I; yet I believe and search Scriptures incredibly every day of my God given life. I fear and respect Him with my whole heart amazing places even in struggles. "Jesus said to them: My food is to do the will of Him who sent Me, and to finish His work. Do you say: There are four months and then comes harvest? Behold, I say lift-up your eyes and look at the fields, for they are already white for harvest! And he who reaps receives wages and gathers fruit for eternal life." **John 4:34-36a**. Jesus explains, and described these things saying.

"That both he who sows and he who reaps may rejoice together." **Verse 36b**. He made the case for all people, so black man; past and present through-out the world. A song writer penned my unseen thoughts entitled: "I Never Would Have Made It Without You in My Life." They say, God carried the writer through inner outer struggles, he delights in Jesus. My first thought is God's will be done my dear readers amazing results leaped in my spirit. A song captivated my mind in the fullness of time. I believed entitled: "DO LORD, DO REMEMBER ME." A taste of my case filled with the joy of God yet no one should to know more about my struggles than God and me. Good or bad we reap and sow I'm getting close to the end of my second chapter the Word says.

"Then they said to the woman: Now we believe, not because of what you said, for we ourselves have heard Him and we know that this is indeed the Christ, the Savoir of the world when the Samaritans." **Verse 42**. As reminders, I always say we ought to know Jesus the Son of God saves. Moving forward, Jesus: "He went to Galilee, the Galileans received Him:" see verse 45.
Without a doubt, I say to my soul, racism rose so high we cannot climb the wall of hatred even in the land of the free. Amazing places even in struggles, so my hope is that we should always remember Jesus healed an anonymous blind man; He didn't even call by name but knew his needs let us not crucify Him again on purpose. Conspicuously I respect our Father, Son, Holy Spirit freely without doubts. "Now as Jesus passed by, He saw a man who was born blind from birth. And His disciples asked Him, saying, Rabbi, who sinned, this man or his parents, that he was born? Jesus said, neither this man or his parents sinned, but that the work of God might be revealed. That long as I am in the world, I am the light of the world." **John 9:1-5**.

As for me, Jesus did not tell His disciples to move on and tend to your own business. So, a question was asked in verse 9 the blind man testified. "He answered and said, A Man called Jesus made clay and anointed my eyes and said to me: Go to the pool of Siloam and wash. So, I went and washed and I received my sight. Then they said to him, where is He? He said, I do not know." **Verses 11-12**. The elders still sang, "This little light of mine I'm going to let it shine." So, let it---- shine. Some elders listened to secular songs 'in the day' titled, "I Pity the Fool." Jesus pities us,

His mercy is forever my beliefs move me onward, for example.

God called to my attention September 21, 2001 between 3 and 5 pm; second chapter God got my complete attention I received a distressed telephone call. My fleshly thoughts were mind blowing suddenly God turned things around abruptly in an hour of my greatest need, He said. "If I will not open for you the windows of heaven, and, pour you out a blessing, that there shall not be room enough to receive it." **Malachi 3:10b**. I knew the place in my Bible, **since the entire verse;** hangs on my south even today works the same; early that Sunday in morning service; I shared when a blessing is too big to receive it. I must share the blessing with others, that is my absolute heart's desire God is my witness. A writer's song entitled: "TRUST, TRY, AND PROVE ME." Words in the song says. "Bring Ye All the tithes into the store-house, All your money, talents, time and love." A charge to keep even in struggles, double blessings. See **Malachi 3:10a**; is famously known as "messenger" A time to shout even in struggle I had a dream.

God said anoint your blue sheets all four corners wash reuse them, I believed Him. It was breathtaking a blessing, I grope through my Bible; I chose Moses testimony said. "Of the blue, and scarlet thread they made garments of ministry, for ministering in the holy place, and made the holy garments for Aaron, as the LORD commanded Moses." **Exodus 39:1**. Moses obeyed God, "He made the ephod of gold, blue, purple and scarlet thread, and fine woven linen, and beat the gold into thin sheets and cut it into threads, to work it in with the blue, purple and scarlet thread, and the fine linen, into artist design. They made shoulder straps for it to couple together at its two edges." **Exodus 39:2-4**. I can't forget my dream stuck in my memory, a God given gift, the ability to remember, my dream itself manifest victory in Jesus I shared it with many others. In my introduction, my royal blue vision is notable, clothe in the mind of Christ is miraculous.

Even so, the breastplate even my royal blue vision, and blue sheet miracle Moses says: "And he made the breastplate, artistically woven like the workmanship of the ephod, of gold, blue, purple, and scarlet thread and of fine linen. They made the breastplate square by doubling it; a span was its length and its width double." **Exodus 39:8-9**. Double blessings are hard to beat. Since God tested, and tried me, the evidence proves my blue sheets miracle. In 2015, a fast became a celebrated feast some family members and I prayed, we approached God fervently together, and use **James 5:16**. That year seemed like Christmas in July year- round, the year I paid of my mortgage God's miracles reminded me How Great IS He. For example, the waters from rain crept like a mighty flood, ready to creep in my house. God said speak to the flood I obeyed Him. Suddenly the waters backed up, God is my witness: it was a blue sheets miracle redeeming the time, a charge to keep even in struggles I sense it is a time to shout even in struggles for Him.

Notably, I enrolled in the community college in my hometown. I selected a course titled the Complete Speaker; after the class ended. Our instructor encouraged me to continue to take more classes. So I listened to the expert, enrolled in other Subjects. After I completed English Comp I, I selected English comp II, which required a ten-page typed essay titled, *The Struggle of a Black Man; Past and Present.* My former English teacher at our school ,Wonder, at that time both husband and wife, we as members of the same church many years she helped pulled resources for my essay. I completed it, my instructor graded my work, B+ my former teacher said it should've been an A+. I sent many thanks to her, for the grade was notably a victory.

Years later, our former teacher and her husband retired after years of excellent work in the in the West Memphis School District. Also, many years of marriage blessed to live in retirement together until her death parted them; may God rest her soul, in spirit her memory lingers on. May God restore and bless her husband health wise; many expert leaders helped many students further their education through college famously. A taste of my essay is very impressive; I heard on the news black women attend college greater today than anyone, a time to shout even in struggles.

Abundantly, I celebrate God's blessings; my two daughters impressed me greatly, continues in higher education: there are many blessings I pray fervently to Him to releases the things I hope. Yet I wait on God. How Remarkable IS HE? As for me, God bring the highest hallelujahs remarkable glancing at Black History repeats itself. "For example, Madame J.C. Walker attended a school in St. Louis Missouri, at night, and early in her career, she invented a metal heating comb and condition for straightening hair. She began as a door to door peddler for her cosmetics eventually amassed a large fortune. She expanded her business to Denver, Colorado, and on to Pittsburgh, Pennsylvania. Then, in 1910 she built a factory in Indianapolis, Indiana, to manufacture her hair preparations, her facial creams and other products." (Taylor 65).

Abundantly, it is remarkable, the situation today is a continuation, in which I use electrical elements, straightening comb, electric curling irons, electric blow dryer, etc. stand up dryer. How remarkable is He? I continue to use these items today; that were door to door peddlers sold. So, struggling with bad hair days it is remarkably good news their wealth increased although afro's these days helps my hair abundantly due to weather reports for example. "Two of the earliest and greatest fortunes among Afro-Americans were made by Annie M. Turnbo Malone and Madame C.J. Walker in the manufacture and marketing of hair preparations for blacks (products such as "Poro" "Heroline," and Black and White). During the first half of the twentieth century." "Funeral services were another personal-service business, almost exclusively under black ownership and control." More abundantly (See Encyclopedia of Black America Edited by W. Augustus Low & Virgil A. Clift, p 201.)

    History is very effective, in which tells the story for us, "Supplying personal services has remained an outstanding of black businesses. Though such, black pursuits as barbering, funeral services still remain almost exclusively for blacks." A charge to keep even in struggles is good feedback. Years later, despite inner outer struggles, remarkably I started to pen this second God breathed book caused great effort, to add or delete certain things I believe to keep me writing.

    On January 4, 2016, the word Prominent leaped in my spirit means famous, admired, people even experts. God is Creator. Jehoiachin was 'released from prison' says: "Now it came to pass in the thirty-seven years of the captivity of Jehoiachin king of Judah, in the twelve months, on the twenty-fifth day of the month, that evil Merodach king of Babylon, in the year of his reign, lifted up his head to him and gave him a prominent seat than those of the kings who were in Babylon, a potion for each until the day of his death, all the days of his life." **Jeremiah 52:31-33.**

God continued favor to the king a taste of His tender loving kindness notice, **II Samuel 9:7, 13.**

To be continued, "Encyclopedia of Black America Edited by W. Augustus Low & Virgil A Clift over 400 illustrations." Notably a wise expert taught black History at West Memphis Senior High, remarkably, till death sweet memories God rest his soul was a very wise prominent man, that I believe gifted by God I asked the price of the book above a couple of others, he delivered the books, told me the price I handed him the money. Excellent investments many prominent Hall of famous people cited in other references, wealthy rich revelations thanks to 'Mr. Cotton.'

"Studies by psychologists and sociologists were cited as support for the statement and segregated schools were harmful to black children (Humphrey 252). After the supreme Court ruled that segregation was un-constitutional, the Arkansas National Guard was brought in to secure peace and order in Central High School in Little Rock, Arkansas before the nine children who were endeavoring to integrate the school were permitted to attend classes, but even then, not without incident (Humphrey 83)." It wasn't kept secret these things show History repeats itself always.

God bless America it's not just my imagination a song titled, "My COUNTRY TIS of THEE." We, the people of America cannot go backward, nor forget our God given freedom. A message from our LORD, my dear readers, healthcare insurances are facts for life on earth Medicare, Medicaid and medical services, if the people stick together work to help enhance the A.C.A. plan instead of repealing it sixty- one times, with intent to cancel it remember, Obama is a prominent man had a message from the LORD to help the brethren he used God's Word asked: "Am I my brother's keeper?" **Genesis 4:9.** Obama invested in this message quietly. God love us 'Black lives matter,' all lives to Him even uninsured people may God bless America get a healthcare plan.

Again, God dropped in my spirit a very prominent wise man. My Bibles says "And Jabez was more honorable than his brethren: and his mother called his name Jabez, saying I bare him with sorrow." **I Chronicles 4:9.** The story intrigues me a charge to keep in struggles, so, I copy these things, because, I too call on the God of Heaven on earth to bless us likewise says. "And Jabez called on the God of Israel, saying Oh that You would bless me indeed, and enlarge my territory, that Your hand would be with me, and that You keep me from evil, that I may not cause pain! God granted his request. **I Chronicles 4:10.** An expert said it is the massage that counts.

"The ideas of liberty and equality expressed so eloquently in the constitution: "ALL MEN ARE CREATED EQUAL," are the very foundation of American Citizenship. Yet, on this issue of equality, freedom and justice, for all, more time, more debate, more bitterness and more bloodshed have focused than on any other single issue on history Cited (Humphrey 91) "For example, even in 1954, two years after the Supreme Court had declared that equal could never be separate, Negro Americans were constantly being reminded that they were no bodies in the only world they knew. That is what Rosa Parks in Montgomery, Alabama: she boarded the bus after a long day of standing on her feet at the department store where she worked as a seamstress."

"Her feet aching and her body tired, Rosa sat down in the vacant seat in the section called, 'the Blind Man's Row.' "This seat in the section could be used by either black or white depending on which end of the bus was more crowded. She sat down thankfully and began reminiscing about last week's sermon by the young vibrant and eloquent young Minister, Rev. King. Her thoughts were interrupted by a stern, threatening voice, "Move back; don't you see a white man standing in the isle?" Mrs. Parks refused the request to the bus driver, and he drove to the next stop, got off the bus hailed a policeman, and of course, the policeman carried her off to jail," (Stern 98).

"So, that incident brought about the formation of a new organization, Montgomery Improvement Association, with Rev. Martin Luther King, Jr. as president." Through peaceful mass action as a means of freeing Negro Americans was not a new concept, it was King through the long years of the boycott in Montgomery who developed peaceful mass action as a technique to tear down that wall that 'Jim Crow' had built" (Stern 109)" Therefore, east, west, north and south inner outer struggles are charges to date; God is our Source by faith, our Protector, the shield rescues us. Eloquently, President Obama, our very first black president served two terms, eight years, my math is not eloquent, but Americans elected him, and God approved him. Son of a white woman and black father is notable to love all people we must all face THE JUDGE individually.

Paul recorded "But if you are led by the Spirit, you are not under the law. Now the works of the flesh are evident, which are adultery, fornication, uncleanness, lewdness, Idolatry, sorcery, hatred, contention, jealousies, outbursts of wrath, selfish ambitions, dissensions, heresies." **Galatians 5:18-20**. Jesus shed His blood for all of us even so. "Envy, murders, drunkenness, revelries, and the like; of which I tell you beforehand, just as I also told you in times past; that those who practice such things will not inherit the kingdom of God. But the fruit of the Spirit is love, joy, peace, long-suffering, kindness goodness, faithfulness." **Galatians 5:21-22**. So, it is a two-way path invest in rich evidences, Paul, reveals true character says. "Gentleness, self-control. Against such there is no law. And those who are Christ's have crucified the flesh with its passions and desires. If we live in the Spirit, let us walk in the Spirit. Let us not become conceited, provoking one another, envying one another." **Galatians 5:23-26**.

      I'm determined to follow and obey God, although a daily test even in struggles Solomon, recorded: "The eyes of the LORD are in every place; Keeping watch on the evil and the good." **Proverbs 15:3**. Yet hope shows more abundantly. The last words say, "The fear of the LORD is the instruction of wisdom, and before honor is humility." **Verse 33**. People young or old should stick together to win over hate, jealousy especially envy, every day He wakes us up. It is written. "And king Solomon loved many foreign women, well as the daughter of Pharaoh: women of Moabites, Ammonites, Edomites, Sidonians and Hittites. From the nations of whom the LORD had said to the children of Israel, you shall not intermarry with them, nor they with you. Surely, they will turn away your hearts after their gods, Solomon clung to these in love." **I Kings 11:1-2**.

      So, it happened as written. "He had seven hundred wives, princesses, and three hundred concubines; and his wives turned away his heart. For it was so, when Solomon was old, that his wives turned his heart after other gods, his heart was not loyal to the LORD as was the heart of his father David." Verses 3-13 see 14-8. God warned Solomon He reveal the consequences of sins says, "And the LORD was angry with Solomon, because his heart turned from the LORD God of Israel, which had appeared to him twice. And had commanded him concerning this thing, that he should not go after other gods; but he did not keep what the LORD had commanded." **Verses 9-10.** Solomon reaped what he sowed as written saying.

"Therefore, the LORD said to Solomon: because you have done this, and have not kept My covenant and My statures, which I have commanded you. I will surely tear the kingdom away from you and give it to your servant. Nevertheless, I will not do it in your days, for the sake of your father David; I will tear it away from your so**n."** **Verses 11-12.** God's mercy endures forever, the way of escape these things. **See Verse 13.** Solomon's story doesn't end here. A charge to keep even in struggles revisit his story therefore read it wow.

Magnificent miracles caught my attention watching T.V. so, I pray for brokenness, pain on faces of children suffering from hungry, sickness and sorrows. I ask God to help them a charge to keep I recall. "A captain of the host of the king of Syria was a great man with his master, and, honorable, because by him the LORD had given deliverance unto Syria. He was also a mighty man in valor, but he was a leper." **II Kings 5:1**. A leper could've been anyone, footnotes said it could've been like AIDS today crushed my spirit. "The Syrians had gone out by companies, and have brought away captive out of the land of Israel a little maid; she waited on Naaman's wife. She said to her mistress, Would God my lord was with the prophet that is in Samaria! For He would recover him of his leprosy." **Verses 2-3.** The power of faith in God **(see verses 4-12).**

"And his servants came near, and spoke to him, and said My father, if the prophet had bid you to do some great thing, would you not have done it? How much rather then, when, he said to you, Wash, and be clean?" **Verses 13.** He believed obeyed in struggles faith works; "Then he went down, and dipped himself seven times in Jordan according to the sayings of a man of God: his flesh came again like the flesh of a little child he was clean." **Verse 14**. Seven is complete. "He returned to the man of God, he and all his aides, and came and stood before him; and he said, indeed, now that there is no God in earth, except in Israel therefore, please take a gift from your servant. **Verse 15**. But Gehazi's plan turned bad Luke the great physical recorded his record says. "Therefore, the leprosy of Naaman shall cling to you and your descendants forever. And he went out from his presence leprous, as white as snow." **Verse 27**.

It is factual like the Word says good or bad we reap what we sow; it happened. "Jesus answered said to them. This is the work of God that you believe in Him whom He sent." **John 6:29**. Amazingly, a question was asked. "They said to Him, what sign will You perform that we may see and believe You? What would you do? Our fathers ate the manna in the desert; as it is written, He gave them bread from heaven to eat. Then Jesus said to them: Most assuredly, I say to you Moses did not give you the bread from heaven, but My Father give the true bread from heaven." **Verses 30-32**. Again, the evidence from above says. "For the bread of God is He who comes down from heaven and gives life to the world. Then they said to Him, LORD give us this bread always. I Am the bread of life." **Verse 35b**. Fast forwarded it happened. "Jesus answered them: Did I not choose you, the twelve, and one of you is a devil?" He spoke of Judas Iscariot, the son of Simon, for it is he who would betray Him, being one of the twelve." **Verse 70-71**.

Consider James, the brother of Jesus exposed hypocrites. A friend says they oppress black farmers, heirs and attempted heirs, James invitation say. "Come now, you rich, weep and howl for your miseries that are coming upon you! Your riches are corrupted, and your garments are moth-eaten. Your gold and silver are corroded, and their corrosion will be a witness against them you and will eat your flesh like fire. You have heaped up treasure in the last days." James 5:1-3; again, I recorded in my first book: and second edition certain things so, I glance back. Black farmers worked years to keep food on their tables to eat; at the end of a year laborers were told nothing was left, families had a place to stay no cash left, because they ate it up, consider. Money isn't needed up yonder or down yonder, "Hope makes not ashamed." See **Romans 5:1-5**.

I must rewrite many hard times we faced back then, and today, black live matter. For its true reminiscing on the Black farmers, heirs and attempted heirs' faithfully file civil rights class action lawsuits; based on years of discrimination. The first trip to Washington D.C. Pigford vs. Glickman 1, reopened to Pigford 2. One day before a five-year statute of limitation expired. Volunteers, our lawyer, black farmers' president, mayors, pastors who called themselves Levites. A prominent woman, a state representative traveled with us, a good thing, for our lawyer to partition Congress in Washington to present our case to lawmakers and other places. The lady helped us immensely. Bus loads from Tennessee, Arkansas, Mississippi other southern states, joined us and we the people volunteered passed it to others made Pigford 2 reopened was great.

Looking to Jesus the second time, more black farmers, their heirs; more busloads of people traveled to Washington for the same purpose we hoped to get paid. The lady went with us again worked being like I said a state rep. Those of us that were able marched, behind a wagon hitched to a mule or two and two men represented forty acres, a mule, and a wagon in the rain joyfully sang. No Justice: No Peace, we want our money! A republican congressman invited black farmers and heirs to Cincinnati, Ohio to its Freedom Underground, to inform black farmers he represented in Ohio to file for their money. We, the black farmers accepted his invitation to help the congressman, we paid our own fare, it was immensely a great place, many people signed up for Pigford 2 a second time, hoped for our money. A time to shout even in struggles.

The black farmers' president's telephone number continued to show up on my phone; a hundred-dollar membership fee annually is key note, to receive after taxes, $50, 000. More money for certain cases continue to farm, the message informs people who desires to omit his calls, press a number and block his number as for me. I don't block it, but pass it on to discriminated people of color since a republican congressman in Arkansas said pay every one of the people, he said black people were discriminated against over a hundred and twenty years God is my witness he said it. We want our money and wait awed-inspired partakers. Four congressmen I know by names, and states they represent, two white republicans, two black democrats continue as lawmakers today. Even so, Jews, Indians etc. got their cash question is when we get ours many have passed away.

An old saying people use says; 'they threw us under the bus.' Yet, the end of the true story hasn't been told nor written; but lawyers on T.V constantly make their commercials sound like billions of black farmers received their cash, but what about us who hired these same lawyers and they accepted the case, so our president filed 20 billion dollars for us the black farmers heirs who tried to file in the eighties. Therefore, I have a charge to keep, never, say never, trust God. I will continue to call out others to state their claims with my law firm application in my file so be it.

Consider Asaph, the author of twelve Psalms said: "Sing out loud to God our strength; Make a joyful shout to the God of Jacob. Raise a song and strike the timbre. The pleasant harp with the lute. Blow the trumpet at the time of the New Moon, at the full moon on our solemn feast day, for this is a statute of Israel, a law of the God of Jacob. He established in Joseph as a testimony," **Psalm 81:1-5a:** So, it is recorded sing out loud 'back in the day' harps, were often instruments made amazing melodies like the timbre-tambourine: today a trumpet is awesomely blown at feast remain absolute says. "When He went throughout the land of Egypt, where I heard a language I did not understand." **5b**. again "Black Lives Matter," for instance Joseph was attacked by his own brothers' innocent people suffer inner out struggles. Therefore, I penned the way of escaped these things Asaph called, and God answered same as I do likewise saying.

"You called in trouble I delivered you; I answered you in the secret places of thunder; I tested you in the waters of Meribah." **Verse 7.** Meribah means 'strife' offended disobedience reminds me of a song that helps me in struggles entitled. "Trouble in My Way I Have to Cry Sometimes." I always tell people cry, but know when to stop. Seek God it works my dear readers, see verses 8-16, it will help, happy or sad He Is God. More abundantly "God stands in the congregation of the mighty; He judges among the gods. How long will you judge unjustly, and show partiality to the wicked? Defend the poor and fatherless; do justice to the afflicted and needy; free them from the hand of the wicked." **Psalm 82:1-4**. A charge to keep even in struggles say; "They do not know nor do they understand;

they walk about in darkness; All the foundations of the earth are unstable. I said You are gods, and all of you are children of the Highest. But you shall die like men, fall like one of the princes. Arise, O God, judge the earth' for You shall inherit all nations." **Verses 5-8**. My task isn't easy, yet its' incredibly, wonderfully, I invest in His good news, hang on to God's wonder working blessings.

Incredible a reporter said on evening news, a tornado was headed east on 1-55 West Memphis, my daughter said her husband heard the news also. But I heard God say, speak to the storm.
I obeyed Him, the storm backed up, God is my witness, I believed Him. A former co-worker lived in Earle called said, the tornado almost torn up the city no one was killed. When dark clouds gather in the sky by faith in God our grandfather split the ground with an axe, the storm passed over, he believed Him absolutely. The first tornado hit West Memphis was the storm of 1987, homes blown down no one was hurt they were rebuilt incredibly, the people in our town God kept us safe; the shield of faith was our protection. Close to my third chapter a time to shout even in struggles, some aging staff we knocked on doors house to house volunteered incredibly.

And we the staff located seniors we served. Carried home delivered meals from Marion kitchen a site in Crittenden provided help to our seniors. A charge to keep even in struggles. How great is our God? Incredibly, the people in our hometown volunteered to help. "Ezekiel's profile say he was not the same after his encounter with God." Question is who is? "Now it came to pass in the thirtieth year, in the fourth month, on the fifth day of the month, as I was among the captives by the River Chebar, that the heavens were opened and I saw visions of God. On the fifth day of the month, which was in the fifth year of king Jehoiachin's captivity, the words of the LORD came expressly to Ezekiel the priest, the son of Buzi as I was among the captives by the River Chebar, and the hand of the LORD was upon him there." **Ezekiel 1:1-3.**

Encounters with God changes my life anew daily; Ezekiel is said to have been "a street preacher" in Babylon 22 years." reminds me after Sunday services, the, witnessed team returned home for personal needs; then we met on the south side of the church prayed for lost souls. One beautiful Sunday evening, the team prayed, walked the streets witnessed to whoever listened. Suddenly we heard gun shots on the street one of our team member lived on; so, ran to her house for safety she called the police. When the policemen arrived, the experts took over abundantly, the team thanked God, the bullets missed us. Ezekiel wrote. "And I looked, and behold, a whirlwind was coming out of the north, a great cloud with raging fire engulfing itself; and brightness was all around it and radiating out of its midst like the color of amber out of the midst of fire." **Verse 4**.

Ezekiel, the prophet of God described his visions; "The likeness of four living creatures. And they had the likeness of a man. Each one had four faces and each one had four wings." **Verse 6**. Fast forwarded says; "The likeness of the firmament above the heads of the living creatures was like the color of awesome crystal, stretched out over their heads." **Verse 24**. God's visions fascinate me, for his visions points to some women of our church enjoyed basketball back in the day. The ladies formed two teams played against each other. Even during my youth, basketball was my favorite game. A basket hanged like a firmament over our heads, the team members bounced the ball in the school gym, tried to score two points to win the game I wondered if Ezekiel had time to play games in his generation; he visualized what he saw and described it.

"Like the appearance of a rainbow in a cloud on a rainy day, so was the appearance of the brightness all around. This was the appearance of the likeness of the glory of the LORD." **Verse 1:28**. The glory of God manifested Ezekiel said: "And He said to me, Son of man I send you to the children of Israel to a rebellious nation that rebelled against Me; they and their fathers have transgressed against Me to this very day." Chapter **2: 3**. God warns His watchmen says. "Whether they hear, or whether they refuse, for they are a rebellious house, yet they shall know that a prophet has been among them." **Verses 4-5**. A song writer penned a top record entitled, "Be Not Dismayed Whatever Betide, God Will Take Care of You." little is known about Ezekiel. "Moreover, He said to me: Son of man, receive into your heart all My words that I speak to you, and hear with your ears. And go, get to the captives, to the children of your people and speak to them, tell them. Thus, says the LORD they will hear or whether they refuse." **Ezekiel 3:10-11**.

So, it happened. "Then the Spirit lifted me up, and I heard behind me a great thunderous voice; Blessed is the glory of God in this place." **Verse 3:12**. Years ago, a friend asked me, did Ezekiel eat human dung? I didn't answer, she would've had to reread chapter four herself. She passed away God rest her soul: I believe sin is the reason God used described as faithful one that obeyed Him Moreover, Ezekiel's visions are clear as pure water I reread charges he acted upon saying. "Lie also on your left side, and lay the iniquity of the house of Israel upon it. For I have laid on you the years of their iniquity, according, to the number of days, three-hundred and ninety days: so, you shall bear the iniquity of the house of Israel. And when you have completed them, lie again on your right side; then you shall bear the iniquity." **Verse 4:4;** see verses **5-8**. It happened imagine, if the people of God had visions and dreams like Ezekiel, even a menu for him recorded says.

"Also take yourself wheat, barley, beans, lentils, millet, and spelt; put them in one vessel, and make bread for yourself. During the number of days that you lie on your side, three hundred and ninety days you shall eat it. And your food which you shall eat by weight, twenty shekels a day, from time to time you shall eat it." **Verse 9-10**. Whatever the charge visions dreams God provided Ezekiel everything needful notable, sin will tell of on us he obeyed God says. "Then He said to me, see I Am giving you cow dung instead of human waste, and you shall prepare your bread over it?" **Verse 15**. I love the book my dear readers, I feel insignificant to express myself I know it is readable for anyone enjoy the prophet and his God given visions. He recorded says. "And when this come to pass, surely it will come, they will know that a prophet has been among them." Ezekiel 33:33. Its' recorded he said, "And the word of the LORD came to me saying. Son of man prophesy against the shepherds of Israel; Wow to the shepherds of Israel who feeds themselves! Should not the shepherds feed the flocks? You eat the fat and clothe yourselves with the wool; you slaughter, the fatlings, but you don't not feed the flock."34:1-3.

"This is the day that the LORD has made I will rejoice and be glad in it." **Psalm 118:24**. A young man's grandma passed, he mourned her death greatly tried to call me. I was unavailable, but He said at that time my voicemail soothed his spirit inside out; the verse above helped people personally for such a time as that. The message remains in my heart, the Word of God helps witness to anyone. We sing today, the song above even I can carry a note titled above. After my own serious thoughts, young millenniums are wise to activate cell phones. See **verses 25-29**. As results, telephone companies, cable television should remember a certain man said rent is to high cut rates get new businesses, speak the truth keep it real be glad inspirit less struggles.

    Paul wrote "Let every soul be subject to the governing authorities. For there is no authority except from God, and the authorities that exist are appointed by God. Therefore, whoever resists the authority resists the ordinances of God, and those who resist the authority resists the ordinances of God, and those who resist will bring judgment on themselves." **Romans 13:1-2**. Government works in down-time, floods, storms we call on God make Him first before time, Paul wrote. "For rulers are not a terror to good works, but to evil. Do you want to be unafraid of the authority? Do what is good and you will have praise of the same. For he is God's minister to you for good. But if you do evil, be afraid; for he does not bear the sword in vain: for he is God's minister, an avenger to execute wrath on him who practices evil." **verses 3-4**.

    Moreover, a famous U.S. Senator said to a journalist on her show, funds were available to those who received Social Security and veterans' benefits. Washington could write a onetime check, only required a vote in Congress, for, no cost of living raise was granted to these participants in 2015. I called the senator's office, her staff person said it was true, I asked a senior to pass on the news to seniors in the sites. Also, I shared the blessing in marketplaces, called our state congressman in Arkansas a clerk said she didn't know anything about the money, she said call Washington, D.C., it didn't work my personal thoughts, consist of forty acres, a mule, and a wagon Congress failed to help us. So, "Therefore, you must be subject, not only to wrath but also for conscience sake. For this cause, you also pay taxes, for they are God's ministers attending continually to this very thing. Render therefore to all their due: taxes to whom taxes, are due, customs to whom customs, fear to whom fear honor to whom honor." **Verses 6-7.**

Therefore, "OWE no man anything except to love one another, for he who loves another has fulfilled the law. For this you shall not commit adultery, you shall not kill nor steal nor bear false witness, nor covet; and if there be any other commandments, it is briefly comprehended in this you shall love your neighbor as yourself." **Verses 8-9**. Paul pass on; "Love does no harm to a neighbor love is the fulfillment of the law: And this do, knowing, the time to awake out of sleep; for now, our salvation is nearer than when we first believed." **Verses 10-11**. Salvation delivers by faith: "The night is far spent the day is at hand. Therefore, let us cast of darkness, and let us walk put on the armor of light. Let us. Let us walk properly, as in the day, not in revelry and not drunkenness, nor in lewdness and lust, not in strife and envy." **Verses 12-13**. constitution is a foundation set to further education, healthcare etc. love all nations seek Him, the shield of faith is fulfilled. "But put on the LORD Jesus Christ, and make no provision for the flesh, to fulfill its lust." **Verse 14.**

Greater than icing on a fresh baked cake. A time to shout even in struggles." Back in the day experts said jobs were sent to foreign countries in early 1990's being in a data computer class it was prophesied in time computers would overtake jobs in U.S.A. right verses wrong so Paul declared. "Receive one who is weak in the faith, but not to dispute over doubtful things, but he who is weak eats only vegetables. Let not him who eats despise him who does not eat, judge him who eats; for God has received him. Who are you to judge another's servant? To his own master he stands or falls. Indeed, he will be mad to stand, for God is able to make him stand. **Romans 14:1-4 see verses 5-15**. "Therefore do not let your good be spoken of as evil, for the kingdom of God in not eating or drinking but righteousness and peace and joy in the Holy Spirit. For he who serves Christ in these things is acceptable to God, approved by men." Verses 16-18. If one has faith, "Happy is he who does not condemned self if he eats or does not." **Verse 22b**.

CHAPTER THREE

"A TIME TO SHOUT EVEN IN STRUGGLES"

Anonymously, a psalmist penned a song of joy so I copy it gladly says. "Shout joyously to the LORD, all the earth: Break forth in song, rejoice, and sing praises. Sing to the LORD with a harp and the sound of a psalm. With trumpets, the sound of a horn; Shout out joyfully before the King. Let the sea roar, and all its fullness the world and all who dwells in it" **Psalm 98:4-7**. Joyfully praising God is magnificent; rejoicing in praises impresses me greatly, I ask myself. How Great IS HE? The psalmist declared God's greatness, continually says. "Let the rivers clap their hands. Let the hills be joyous together before the LORD. For He is coming to judge the earth, with righteousness He shall judge the world, and the peoples with equity." Verse 8-9.

There rivers make a joyful noise, the waves roll over rejoiced down by the river side: a time to shout even in struggles. A Psalm of the sons of Korah inaction recorded. "O clap your hands, all you people! Shout to God with the voice of triumph! For the LORD, Most High is awesome: He is King over the earth. He will subdue the people under us, the nations under our feet. He will choose our inheritance for us, the excellence of Jacob whom He loves. God has gone up with a shout, the LORD with the sound of a trumpet." **Psalm 47:1-5**. Every living soul and anyone that passed away should know God deserves our praises; "For God is King of all the earth; Sing praises with understanding. God reigns over the nations: God sits on the throne. The princes of the people have gathered together, the people of the God of Abraham. For the shields of the earth belong to God; He is greatly exalted." **Verses 7-9**. Amazingly rivers stand still at His command.

Abraham, Jacob and Isaac, knew the shield of faith protected them saying. "Now to Abraham and his Seed were the promises made. He does not say, and to seeds, as of many, but as of one: And to your Seed, who is Christ. And this I say, that the law, which was four hundred and thirty years later, cannot annual the covenant that was confirmed before by God in Christ, that is should be made the promise of no effect." **Galatians 3:16-17**. God spoken Word opens my God given eyes to see ears to listen say. "For the inheritance is of the law, it is no longer of promise but God gave it to Abraham by promise. What than does the law serve? It was added because of transgressions, till the Seed should come to whom the promise was made; and it was appointed through angels by the hand of the mediator. Now a mediator does not mediate for one only, but God is One." **Verses 19-20**. A mediator acts as a peacemaker between two or more people to settled disputes. Paul wrote abundantly clear, "Is the law then against the promises of God? Certainly not! For if there had been a law given which could have given life, truly righteousness would have been by the law. But the Scripture has confined all under sin that the promise by faith in Jesus Christ might be given to those who believe." **Verses 21-22**.

The Word of God miraculously says, "But before faith came, we were kept under guard by the law, kept for the faith, which afterward be revealed. Therefore, the law was our schoolmaster to bring us to Christ, that we might be justified by faith. But after faith has come, we are no longer under a tutor." **Verses 23-25**. Miraculously, a song writer penned a song, "We Come This Far by Faith." So, the children of God connect with Him. **Verses 26-27a**.

"Baptized into Christ have put on Christ. There is neither male nor female; for you are all one in Christ Jesus. And if you are Christ's, then you are Abraham's seed, and heirs according to His promise." **Verses 27b-29**. Children are included by faith as heirs. "Now faith is the substance of things hoped for, the evidence of things not seen. For by it the elders obtained a good testimony. By faith we understand the worlds were framed by the Word of God. So that the things which are seen were not made of things which are visible." **Hebrews 11:1-3**. For God is invisible same as faith.

Asaph described amazingly, "The Mighty One, God the LORD has spoken and called the earth from the rising of the sun to its going down. Out of Zion, the perfection of beauty, God will shine forth. Our God shall come, and shall not keep silent, a fire will devour before Him and it shall be very tempestuous all around Him." **Psalm 50:1-3, verses 4-9**. God said, "For every beast of the field is Mine, and the cattle of a thousand hills. I know all the birds of the mountains the wild beast of the field is Mine. If I were hungry, I would not tell you; for the world is Mine, and its fullness." **Verses 10-12**. These things work. see **verse 13**, "Offer God thanksgiving, and pay your vows to the, Most High God. Call upon Me in the day of trouble; I will deliver you, and you shall glorify Me." **Verses 14-15**. Mighty God point to LORD who has no beginning nor end. Regardless of our names He knows good or bad none can fool Him. So, Jesus made a way to escape inner outer struggles two-way questions says; "But to the wicked God says what right have you to declare My statures, or take My covenant in your mouth." **Verse 16**. He says to us, "Seeing you hate instruction and cast My words behind you? You give your mouth to evil, and your tongue frames deceit. You speak against your brother; you slander your own mother's son. These things you have done I kept silent; you thought I was altogether like you; I rebuke you, set them in order before your ears. **Verses 19-21**. Who will obey God?

"Now consider this, you who forget God, Lest I tear you in pieces, and there be none to deliver." **Verse 22**. Again, consider is a word from above to think and observe because a verse shows three ways to please God saying. "Whoever offers praise glorifies Me; and to him who orders his conversation aright, I will show the salvation of God." **Verse 23**. A woman of faith knew for sure I walked the streets in our hometown shared with saved and unsaved people these things says. "Not forsaking the assembling of ourselves together, as the matter of some, but exalting one another, and so much as you see the Day approaching." **Hebrews 10:25.** But her voice wasn't "exalting one another," or encouraging in the presence of other so I quoted, the above **Psalm 50:23**. For salvation, is God's gift to the world, Jesus saves by the power of His blood the writer unnamed gazing back is rooted deed **Hebrews 10:19-21.**

Now consider these things, "Therefore, brethren, having boldness to enter the Holiest by the blood of Jesus: by a new and living way when He consecrated for us the veil, that is His flesh, and having a High Priest over the house of God. Let us draw near with a true heart in full assurance of faith, having our hearts sprinkled from an evil conscience and our bodies washed with pure water." I practice boldly in the streets or marketplaces. "Let us hold fast to the confession of hope without wavering, for He who promised is faithful. And let us consider one another to stir up love and good works." Verses **22-24**. He made a promise in a song the song writer penned, what I do daily a verse say, "Ask the Savior to help you. He will carry you through." Therefore, "Vengeance is Mine, I will repay, says the LORD.

And again, the LORD will judge His people. It is a fearful thing to fall into the hands of the Living God. But recall the former days in which, after you were illuminated, you endured a great struggle with sufferings." **verses 30-32**. Face to face struggles continues God is faithful. The way to escape these things refreshes me, it is a time to shout even in struggles see verse 33-34. I shout to exalt our God highly. "Therefore, do not cast away your confidence, which have great reward, For, you have need of endurance, after you have done the will of God, you may receive the promise:" verses 35-36. The voice of God even struggling says. "Yet a little while, and He who is coming will come and will not tarry. Now the just shall live by faith." **Hebrews 10:37-38a**. See **38a-39**. I move on, "the just shall live by faith." A time to shout even in struggles.

Isaiah declared these things saying, "So, shall My Word that goes out of My mouth; it shall not return to Me void, But, shall accomplish what I please, and it shall prosper in the thing for which I sent it." **55:11**; "For you shall go out with joy, and be led with peace; the mountains and hills shall break into singing before you, and all the trees of the field shall clap their hands." **Isaiah 55:12**. I blessed God and point out it's a time to shout in amazing places, because the truth is out, same as a lie. Yet, His Word never returns void see the abundant life lessons on earth must be fulfilled, is His will, to be continued because it is the Word, only believe these things always.

"When Solomon had finished praying, fire came down from heaven and consumed the burnt offerings and sacrifices; and the glory of the LORD filled the temple." Written in **II Chronicles 7:1.** An old Doctor Watt our dear mother sang people sing today says: "Fire keeps on burning, I can't hold my peace." All Israel noticed the fire.

Yet struggles encircled me like a ring on my finger, yet in due season He added more to my book. Solomon used dates and place throughout his own assignments. For example, he said. "On the twenty-third day of the seventh month he sent the people away to their tents, joyful and glad of heart for the good that the LORD had done for David, for Solomon and His people Israel: Solomon finished the house of the LORD and the king's house; and Solomon successfully accomplished all that came into his heart to make in the house of the LORD and in his own house." **Verses 10-11**. I believe the people kept on praying.

A generational Hymnal entitled: "A CHARGE TO KEEP I HAVE," A God to Glorify Who Gave His Son, My Soul to Save: Fit It from The Sky to Serve: The Present Age My Calling to Fulfill. "It is written. "Then the LORD appeared to Solomon by 'night,' and He said to him; I have heard your prayers, and have chosen this place for Myself as a house of sacrifice. When I shut up heaven and there is no rain, or command the locusts to devour the land, or send pestilence among My people." **Verses 12-13**. Solomon penned breathtaking miracles, acts, signs, the works; repeated amazing requests charges to keep, God said. "If My people who are called by My name will humble themselves, and pray and seek my face, and turn from their wicked ways, then I will hear from heaven, and will forgive their sin and heal their land." **Verse 14**.

For instances, in the great city of Flint Michigan. The people cried out for help and a little girl lives in the city wrote to President Obama for help. A time to shout even in struggles, a child was concerned about lead in their water. So, I watched television and prayed for them, also all cities and states pipes need checked or replaced because of infected erosion pipes. More abundantly, a certain Journalist intervened who work very hard, host of her show spoke out on Lead was in the water in Flint MI. So, world news got the message, and many concerned citizens, east, west, north, and south the word was out, and the people pitched in to help the people in Flint. Many cities acted as water carriers, so, the people of U.S.A, and flint MI prayed.

Moreover, my two sisters abide in Michigan; one in Flint for many years and one in Detroit likewise. Friends of mine continue to live in Flint Michigan. A journalist, host of her television show, says often, "watch the space." It happened, broadcasters' other news reporters passed it on; many people invested in the evidence. Train young people also realized true facts of life produces great skills. Moreover, God charged Solomon and promised him says. "And I will establish the throne of your kingdom, as I covenanted with David your father, saying: You shall not fail to have a man as ruler over Israel." **Verse 18**. Looking back again, although it didn't make news at that time. A certain young man, a member of the church telephoned me at midnight abruptly, and said, had I not answered my phone, he would've shot himself to death. I was speechless.

But God opened my mouth to witness to him I said He loves you, and canceled a death notice at midnight for you! Inner outer struggles almost cost him his God given life. I talked to him until daylight on our telephones famously, God's amazing love, grace, and mercy plan works by Him power. Solomon wrote, "A righteous man may fall seven times and rise again, But the wicked shall fall by calamity." **Proverbs 24:16**. It was a time to shout even in struggles God made a way to escape death, he found my number listed in the book abruptly. A king in his generation, "That night king Ahasuerus couldn't sleep. So, one was commanded to bring the book of records of chronicles; and they were read before the king. And it was found written that Mordecai had told of Bigthana and Teresh, two of the king's eunuch's, the door-keepers who sought to lay hand on king Ahasuerus." **Esther 6:1-2**. God preapproved a plan I believe by His power beforehand it is said the author, possibly Mordecai, **see 9:29**.

"Then the king said, what honor or dignity has been bestowed on Mordecai for this? And the king's servant who attended him said, nothing has been done for him. So, the king said, who is in the court? Now Haman had just entered the outer court of the king's palace to suggest that the king hang Mordecai on the gallows that he prepared for him." **Esther 6:3-4**. I believe the time had come for Mortdecai's reward, "The king's servant said to him, Haman is there, standing in the court, and the king said, let him come in. So, Haman came in, and the king asked him what shall be done for the man whom the king delights to honor? Now Haman thought in his heart, whom would the king delight to honor more than me?" **Verses 5-7**. Yet struggles begin for Haman. Because, the king said. "Let a royal robe be brought which the king has worn, and a horse on which the king has ridden, which has a royal crown placed on his head." **Verse 8**. For example, the king's orders points to I **King 1:33-37**, Solomon's inauguration. So, the king, Ahasuerus approved orders say "Then let this robe and horse be delivered to the hand of one of the king's most noble princes, that he may array the man whom the king delights to honor. Then parade him on horseback through the city square, and proclaim before him; Thus, shall it be done to the man the king delights to honor!" **Esther 6:9**. Haman obeyed his orders. See **verses 10 -14**.
.
Howbeit, the gallons were hand made for Haman to hang himself instead of Mordecai chapter 7. I thought about a shield of faith, my God given vision revealed to a woman of faith said He desired me to dress head to toe in royal

blue, she didn't hesitate I searched the Scriptures clothed with the mind of Christ. An anonymous psalmist recorded. "Our soul waits for the LORD: He is our help and our shield." **Psalm 33:20**. The sons of Korah wrote; "O God, behold our shield, and look upon the face of Your anointed." **Psalm 84:9**. A time to shout even in struggles. If millennials whatever creed, 'a system of religious belief,' race, gender, rich or poor, work for our Most-High know Jesus, our King the Royal One; obey Him, like an anonymous writer says.

"And king Ahasuerus imposed tribute on the land and on the islands of the sea. Now all the acts of his power, his might and the account of the greatness of Mordecai, to which the king advanced him, are they not written in the book of the chronicles of the kings of Media and Persia?" **Esther 10:1-2**. The evidence says; "For Mordecai, the Jew was second to king Ahasuerus, and great among the Jews and well received by the multitude of his brethren, seeking the good of his people, speaking peace to all his countrymen." **Verse 3**. Mordecai' reaped greatly private and openly he rode on the king's horse-back wore his royal, dress in his apparels as a prominent man I believe God released to help me write and complete my book is my belief.

Consider God raised up prominent people that struggled says. "Then after some days Paul said to Barnabas, let us now go back and visit our brethren in every city where we have preached the word of the LORD, and see how they are doing, Now Barnabas was determined to take with him John called Mark, But Paul insisted that they should not take with them one who had departed from them in Pamphylia and had not gone with them to work." **Acts 15:36-38**. Believers disagree at times it is written, saying "Their contention became so sharp that they parted from one another. And Bananas took Mark and sailed to Cypress; but Paul chose Silas and departed, being commented by the brethren to the grace of God. And he went through Syria and Cilicia, strengthening the churches." **Verses 39-41**. Even struggling things worked out, "to the grace of God." My dear readers, purified revelations straight from His breathtaking Word captured my mind completely for life absolutely, a vision from the words below, as written says.

"And at midnight Paul and Silas prayed, to God: and the prisoners heard them. And suddenly there was a great earthquake so the foundations of the prison were shaken and immediately all the doors were open, and every one's bands were loosed." **Acts 16:25-26**. A young man close to my heart faced great struggles at that time. Allegedly, his case was filed in court four charges against him. God is my witness! The above Scripture was my confidence His vision happened even before his court date. So, a young lady and I arrived in court to listen to the judge's report. I glanced across the room noticed a lawyer who looked like he knew how to handle himself in a courtroom. And said to her I need to talk to that lawyer, suddenly to my complete surprise, she knew him personally. Later, I made an appointment with the lawyer and met him face to face.

Because I trusted God in that He revealed visions and dreams and spoke openly to Him. I introduced myself to him quoted God's Word to him above. Nothing but the truth so, help me God and stuck to His Word. I made my case to the lawyer said if the young man had been guilty with a gun in his hand, he would've been shot to death instantly, as a young black man in the first place. Absolutely without a doubt in my heart, the lawyer investigated the case, after- ward he said he hoped my prophesy was accurate. It was. I heard His Word; then he said he was a Christian also. So, later the same year, a second time, he returned to court as did the young man. I didn't go. That next Tuesday morning, at 10:00 a.m.—my favorite time of the day—my telephone rang. The young man said the judge dropped all four charges. I shouted out loud! God made *The Way of Escape These Things* for him. But his true story was a three-part specialized story straight from God, too hard for man to fix, just right for God the absolute truth.

      The young man refreshed himself God revived him. His favorite chapter is **Psalm 91:1-16**. An anonymous psalmist penned a conspicuous revival story immensely great saying. "He that dwells in the secret place of the Most-High shall abide under the shadow of the Almighty, I will say of the LORD, He is my refuge and my fortress: my God; in Him will I trust. Surely, He shall deliver you from the snare of the fowler, and from the noisome pestilence. He shall cover you with His feathers, and under His wings shall thou trust:" **Psalm 91:1-4a**. His truth shall be my Shield." **Verse 4b**. He is our, 'shield of faith.' David says: "Take hold of the shield and buckler: And stand up for my help. Also draw out the spear, stop those who pursue me, say to my soul, I am your salvations. Let them be shamed that brought me to dishonor:" **Psalm 35:2-4a**

      Openly God delivered the young man. His intentions stood strong for him, for the lady in charge of his case, her name was Mrs. Shields! His Word says: "You shall not be afraid of terror by night; nor the arrow that flies by day; nor for the pestilence that walks in darkness; nor for the destruction that waste at noonday. A thousand shall fall at your right side; but it shall not come near you." **Psalm 91: 5-7**. God's secret place hides us personally I called a "Shield" in Him show out for believers' unseen radical faith inaction protects and defends us before, a storm, during a storm and knew after a storm. I trust Him even in inner outer struggles. So, the unnamed psalmist writer known to God had a charge to keep continues to all generations manifest; A time to shout even in struggles Jesus, knows our names, whosoever believes: "For He will give His angles charge over you, to keep you in all your ways." **Verses 8-11**. A time to shout even in struggles. A song writer penned my own thoughts entitled, "O to be Kept by God." The writer penned: "They shall bear you up lest you dash your foot against a stone. You shall tread upon the lion and cobra and the adder: the young lion and the dragon shall trample underfoot." **Verses 12-13**. God strengthens His people even a thousand shall fall at your feet

"Because he has set his love upon Me therefore I will deliver him; I will set him on high, because He has known My name. He shall call upon Me and I will answer him; I will be with him in trouble; I will deliver him and honor him: With long life, I will satisfy him show him My salvation." **Verses 14-16**. A time to shout even in struggles; revisit **Psalm 91**: while penning this report, an expert journalist I watch on T.V. had a charge to keep, said he had to "Eulogize" an aunt, her name was "Mrs. Shields!" It was a three-fold time to shout even in struggles. The young man testified in the year 2005 God called him to teach. I know three-fold reasons none hide, or run, from Him, for. God is our Father, Jesus is His Son, Holy Spirit is our Comforter. The young man run track, won prizes, placed football, even so God said to him. "I beseech you therefore, brethren, by the mercies of God, that you present your bodies a living sacrifice, holy acceptable to God, which is your reason service." **Romans 12:1**. A time to shout even is struggles.

"And do not conformed to this world, but be transformed by the renewing of your mind, that you may prove what is a good and acceptable and perfect will of God. For I say by the grace given to me, to everyone who is among you, not to think of himself more highly than he ought to think, but to think soberly, as God has dealt to each one a measure of faith." **Verses 2-3**. That very moment, I witnessed, hidden things points to Jeremiah passed on, **33:3**, says, "Call unto Me, and I will answer you, and show you great and mighty things, which you do not know." God's power, my belief is purified in Him. David penned, I lay down and slept; I awoke, for the LORD sustained me. I will not be afraid of ten-thousands of people who had set themselves against me all around." **Psalm 3:5-6**, David said, "Salvation belongs to the LORD. Your blessing is upon His people." **Verse 8**. Even struggling He is faithful since faith is unseen same as God IS!

I met a young lady that looked familiar to me; I asked what her name was. She informed me I was her substitute teacher at West Memphis Senior High School years ago. I remembered she was a former classmate of my granddaughter, because some students imitated my grandson and granddaughter called me granny, even today. I greet some in market-places, churches good to be remembered. I asked the young lady if she knew any authors in our hometown. She referred at that very moment, Katrina Avant. She edited and published my second edition the way to escape these things. Katrina said she handed her a business card she forgot it, then informed me her first book was like a draft, but she didn't quit writing. Today she writes, edits, publishes books within our hometown through her publishing company, Katrina's Works Publishing LLC. Katrina is the daughter of a former Wonder High student a good thing! And her referrals are great.

More abundantly, I told the Katrina the truth my desire is to continue use two words: these things. The Word helps me to write my books; less clichés, is the way to escape struggles what I know, but who is Him. Regardless of where we live, my dear readers, east, west, north or south, in unity, in humility, everyone under the sun is tested abundantly; a time to shout even in struggles it was a time to shout out praises to God. Solomon explained these things in his older years learned greater things said. "For I considered all this in my heart. So that I could declare it all: that the righteous and the wise and their works are in the hand of God. People neither love nor hatred by anything they see before them. All things come alike to all. One event happens to the righteous and the wicked; to the good, the clean and the unclean." **Ecclesiastes 9:1-2a**.

I believe these things Solomon talks about everyone says. "I returned and saw under the sun that; The race is not to the swift, Nor the battle to the strong, nor bread to the wise, nor riches to men of understanding: Nor favor to men of skill: But time and chance happens to them all." Eccl. 9:11b. Consider A certain foreigner struggled shown on T.V. he cried out loud, because lawmen hand cupped sent him back to a foreign land his wife had cancer, as her caretaker, once upon a time I wept for them being an experienced caregiver. I asked God to help them through painful struggles, and shared with some ladies, having lunch together these things fill me up with pity people struggling I considered; "He's Got the Whole World in His Hand." **See Eccl: 9:12-16**.

Solomon said, "Words of the wise, spoken quietly, should be heard rather than the shout of a ruler of fools. Wisdom is better than weapons, of war, but one sinner, destroys much goods." **Eccl 9:17-18**. Again, watching T.V. a mother deported from her family sent back to Mexico her daughter struggled sadly talked about their loss reminds me of Jeremiah a weeping prophet wrote. "I would comfort myself in sorrow; my heart is faint in me. Listen! The voice, the cry of the daughter of my people from a far country: Is not the LORD in Zion: Is not her King in her?" **Jeremiah 8:18-19**. The prophet said: "The harvest is past; the summer is ended: And we are not saved!" **Verse 20**. The prophet's emotions reveal sorrow for the people in the first place.

"For the heart of my daughter of my people I am hurt. I am mourning: Astonishment has taken hold of my people, is there a balm in Gilead, Is there a physician there? Why is there no recovery for the health of the daughter of my people? **Verses 21-22**. The prophet's suffering point to these things. A certain wise woman desired to fix healthcare make it better for the people of U.S.A. I believed her; again, God said ACA would prosper I stick to faith in Him. "But as it is written, Eye has not seen, nor ear heard, nor have entered into the heart of man the things which God has prepared for those who love Him? But God has revealed to us through His Spirit. For the Spirit searches all things. Yes, the deep things of God." **I Corinthians 2:9-10**. I get it a time to shout even in struggles, deep in my soul, testify and know I can't breathe without Him.

"Now we have received, not the spirit of the world, but the Spirit who is from God, that we might know the things that have been freely given to us by God." **Verses 11**. No one measures the Spirit or deep things but God our Father, Son and Spirit; my ears are open to refresh myself anew reminds me Solomon penned, "The spirit of man is the lamp of the LORD: Searching all the inner depths of his heart. Mercy and truth preserve the king, and by loving kindness he upholds his throne." **Proverbs 20:27-28**.

Backyard Bible clubs captured my attention. A couple, man and wife, invested in it; some clubs continue today.

Glancing back, a friend needed help asking me to assist her as host in her backyard club for little children within her neighborhood. I agreed in doing so. I learned the process and hosted a club in my backyard eighteen years after; every summer for a week with kids in our area. My daughter added one year at her home with a total of nineteen years which were a great joy to me. Kids accepted Christ with the help of my faithful family friends and helpers, immensely. My dear friend passed away. In sweet memory of her I remember her as a faithful woman of God; excellent company and such a woman of faith, God be the glory.

Jesus declared, "Take heed that you despise not one of these little ones; for I say to you, that in heaven their angles always see the face of My Father which is in heaven. For the Son of man is come to save that which was lost. What do you think? If a man has a hundred sheep, and one of them goes astray, does he not leave the ninety-nine and go to the mountains to seek the one that is straying." **Matthew 18:12**.

In the process, the first Sunday in January 2007, God spoke to me exceedingly awe-inspired inside out said. He said if My people praise, worship and celebrate Him the first seven days in the New Year, whoever does these things would prosper, the entire year. I was so excited I could barely wait to share with early morning worshipers in service. My pastor at that time asked what Scripture did God reveal to me to celebrate Him? I said, **Leviticus 23.** He was satisfied. A member of the mother's board, a friend of mine, said she would celebrate Him according to His Word to me the first seven days in the year 2007.

Absolutely with purified glee, other members present from other churches confirmed God said the same things to them, celebrate Him. That year seemed like God "Bore you on eagle's wings" and brought you to Myself." **Exodus 19:4b**. God is my witness, when one works for Him who keeps up with time?

Fast forwarded. Overwhelmed with the joy of God, the first Sunday in 2008, the same mother walked in early service confessed she celebrated God the first seven days in 2007, glee in her voice that year turned out to be absolutely the best year of her entire life. As a result, her face glowed in likeness of a huge diamond ring on her finger. I was glad to be in the place to hear her absolute amazing testimony; a time to shout out to God; a widow at that time. Later with glee in her voice she wore a diamond wedding ring on her finger, she got married!

An unnamed psalmist's request said; "Praise the LORD! Blessed is the man who fears the LORD: Who delights greatly in His commandments. His descendants will be mighty on earth: The generation of the upright will be blessed. Wealth and riches will be in his house, and His righteousness' endues forever." **Psalms 112:1-3**. Top of the mountain blessings cause praise leaders to testify about Him saying; "Unto the upright there arises light in darkness; He is gracious and full of compassion, and righteous. A good man deals graciously and lends; He will guide his affairs with discretion: Surely he will never be shaken; the righteous will be in everlasting remembrance." **Verses 4-6.** struggles do not last always so I praise Him.

This is not the end of the true story the verdict says: "He will not be afraid of evil tidings; His heart is steadfast trusting in the LORD. His heart is established; He will not be afraid, until he sees his desire upon his enemies; He has dispersed abroad, He had given to the poor; His righteousness endures forever, His horn will be exalted with honor." **Verses 7-9**. It is always a time to shout and leap for joy none of us deserves the grace of God. A psalmist debated a good case to stick to. The Bible describes that "Wicked people will not see it and be grieved; He will gnash his teeth and melt away, the desire of the wicked will perish." **Verse 10**.

Yet, I just praise God, because an unnamed palmist's record is established forever by His power and I believe every word saying. "From the rising of the sun to its going down the LORD'S name is to be praised. The LORD is high above all nations His glory above the heavens: Who is like the LORD our God who dwells on high: Who humbles Himself to behold the things that are in the heavens and in the earth?" **Psalm 113: 3-6**. Humbly, my first book aimed to help others in struggles: "He raises up the poor out of the dust, and lifts the needy out of the ash heap, that He may seat him with princes: With the princes of His people. He grants the barren woman a home, like a joyful mother. Praise the LORD." **Verses 7-9**. A time to shout even in struggles.

Jeremiah got a massage from the LORD to pass the reason for struggles: "If, you will return, O Israel, says the LORD, Return to Me; and if you put away your abominations out of My sight. Then you shall not be moved. And you shall swear. The LORD lives in truth, judgment and righteousness, the nations shall bless themselves in Him they shall glory." **Jeremiah 4:1-2**. These things remind me, back in the day many of us chopped cotton, worked the gardens. In fact, the elders said, if they did not raise anything, they didn't eat. Nothing came in to help them, nothing went out. "For thus said the LORD to the men of Judah and Jerusalem: break up your fallow ground, and do not sow among thorns. Circumcise yourselves to the LORD. And take away the foreskins of your hearts, you men of Judah and inhabitants of Jerusalem. Lest my fury come forth like fire." **Verses 3-4a**. God is a heart. He sees all things to pass it on again. Jeremiah wrote the consequences to disobeying God: "And burn so that no one can quench it, because of the evil of your doings." **Verses 4b see verses 5-30; 31**. These verses tells of a woman in labor.

Moreover, back in the day women laid awake in pain and sorrow. Midwives did the best they could to deliver babies. We were told a strong one delivered two of us, my twin brother; I came out first an hour apart. Again, I stick to these things. My best friend since third grade said at age fourteen, my heart's desire was to become a writer. I don't remember, at that time our dear sweet wonderful dear mother passed away with breast cancer. God rested her from all her pain and sorrow. Inner outer struggles began; I still feel the pain. I tried to pull our mother back to life. God loved and knew she suffered in much pain and sorrow. I remember, the four of us waving at her from her hospital bed, a song we sing today title "If I couldn't say a word, I'll just wave my hand, I recorded in my first and second editions, moreover God gives us breaks from struggles.

My friend from third grade was right, because I read *True Story books* to ease my broken heart. Many years passed and my best friend passed away. Although I read a portion of my book to her, because she always said she would market my book, she knew it wasn't about me, but Him. I remember she testified that her God would not allow her to suffer a long time. I used Solomon: "Death and life are in the power of the tongue, and who love it will eat the fruit thereof." **Proverbs 18:21**. I asked her to speak life until God calls her home and she obeyed. Gazing back, I penned this anonymous psalmist record first, since it tells true life family stories. "Blessed is everyone who fears the LORD, who walks in His ways. When you eat the labor of your hands, you shall be happy, and it shall be well with you. Your wife shall be like a fruitful vine in the very heart of your house, your children like olive plants all around your table." **Psalm 128:1-3**.

A professional and former student of our school Wonder made his saxophone talk. He was an expert musician. I believe God called Him to preach and he obeyed. Later church members called him, "the baptizer." Like a crop produces abundantly good things to eat, the unnamed writer said, "Behold, thus shall the man be blessed who fears the LORD. The LORD blesses you out of Zion. And may you see the good of Jerusalem All the days of your life. Yes, may you see your children's children. Peace be upon Israel!" **Verses 4-6**.

Isaiah, chosen by God was said to be rich in "Messianic references, preeminently, the prophet of redemption his name means Salvation of Jehovah." Husband, and father of two sons their names are listed in his book, his famous story manifested to the world he asked. "Who has directed the Spirit of the LORD? Or His counsel, and who instructed Him, and taught Him in the path of Justice? Who taught Him knowledge, and showed Him the way of understanding? **Isaiah 40:13-14**. The record said, "Behold, the nations are as a drop in a bucket and are counted as the small dust on the scale." **Verse 15**. Consider these things Isaiah wrote; "It is He who sits above the circle of the earth, and its inhabitants are like grasshoppers, who stretches out the heavens like a certain, and spreads them out like a tent to dwell." **Verse 22**. How great is our Mighty God?

The first time I flew on an airplane, I sat next to a window as it ascended in the sky. I looked down and everything looked like grasshoppers. Our Creator encircles every one of us in likeness of a ring on our fingers. Like some hats cover our heads in likeness of bad hair days. A song writer penned "I Say Wait on the LORD." Isaiah penned top questions good to my taste. "Have You not known? The everlasting God, the LORD, The Creator of the earth, neither faints nor is weary. His understanding is unsearchable: He gives power to the weak." **Verse 28**.

A young black man was shot to death in our hometown. He wasn't alone. One very close to my heart said they were getting ready to party with close friends when it happened. Because the preacher took his text, I spoke comfort to his family and friends; the way to escape these things is to return to God. I used Isaiah's words: "He gives power to the weak and those who have no might He increases strength. Even the youths shall faint and be weary, and the young men shall utterly fall; but those that wait on the LORD Shall renew their strength; they shall mount up with wings like eagles. They shall run and not be weary. They shall walk and not faint." **Verses 29-31**.

Refreshingly, it was a charge to shout even in struggles marvelously. God is the strength of life all lives and black lives matter to Him; consider these things. "Produce your cause, said the LORD; bring forth your strong reason, said the King of Jacob. Let them bring forth show us what shall happen: let them show former things, what shall they be, then we may consider them, and know the latter end of them or declare us things to come." **Isaiah 41:21-22**.

A song writer penned a song titled "Take Me to The King." Years ago, bored with the same old things, I shared it with my former pastor, like people use nut crackers to burst open nuts. Refreshed in Him he cracked my boredom acts wide open and said go minister to those peoples in the nursing homes. I said to myself, he is a wise man that's what I get for complaining and accepted his charge. So I called an elderly lady and invited her to go with me. She was delighted. As a result, unless hindered by reasons, we witnessed thirteen years together in the nursing home. We sang, prayed and listen to the people testify. At Christmas, she gave me a card with ten dollars; I didn't charge her! She said don't cut your blessing off. Is that possible, a widow's fixed income? So, I remember the words of Jesus, "Truly I say to you this poor widow has put in more than all." **Luke 21:3**.

A young lady said she watched me enter church praising God. If she knew my struggles she would shout daily, and mark the psalmist says: "Make a joyful shout to the LORD, all you land!" **Psalm 100:1-5**. I wrote the above, entire psalm in my first book fresh from the heart. David said, "Even there Your hand shall lead me. And your right hand shall hold me up." **Psalm 139:10**. I also copied **139 Psalm** also in my first books and second edition. January 31st a young lady who baby sat for me 'back in the day', to make it plain, the two of us continue to be prayer warriors; rejoicing excitedly glad to be in the land of the living, the last of the month above. She said she was caught up in the Spirit in hopes to witness a brand-new year in the LORD. She led a song, and honestly said she didn't know where it came from, neither did I, that was her story she blessed Him afresh.

An unknown writer declared, "You have persecuted me without a cause; but my heart stands in awe of Your Word. So, I rejoice at Your Word, as one that finds great spoil. I hate and abhor lying; but Your law, do I love."

Psalm 119:160-163. I've always loved the words, a time to shout in struggles. Also, I love saying: "Seven times a day do I praise You, because of Your righteous judgments, Great peace have they which love Your law: And nothing causes them to stumble. LORD I hope for Your salvation. And I do Your commandments." **Psalm 119:164-166**.

The seventh month is completeness, my God given revelations sticks in my spirit today. So then, before a young lady was conceived in her mom's womb, or landed in her mom's arms. Years later her daughter had serious surgery, at the appointed her doctor advised her to get out of bed walk, her mom said she didn't obey him. God said to me, run, shout hallelujah in every room seven times for her healing. I just obeyed Him. The next day we went to the hospital and when I entered her room she got up and walked. I had a charge to keep; the power of God works number seven also. GOD IS SOMETHING ELSE. The writer wrote: "My soul keeps Your testimonies, And I love them exceedingly. I keep Your percepts and Your testimonies for my ways are before You." **Verses 167-168**.

One of Jesus' disciples was in a struggle, may have been his purpose says. "Now Thomas, called the Twin, one of the twelve, was not with them when Jesus came. The other disciple therefore said to him, we have seen the LORD. So, he said to them, Unless I see in His hands the print of the nails, and put my finger into the print of the nails, and put my hand into His side, I will not believe." **John 20:24-25.** Consider Thomas' unbelief, "After eight days His disciples were inside, and Thomas was with them. And said, Peace to you!" **Verse 26**. My dear I see miracles for doubters. "He said to Thomas, reach your finger here, look at My hands; and reach your hand here and put it into My side. And be not faithless but believing. And Thomas answered and said to Him, My LORD and my God! Jesus said to him, Thomas, because you have seen Me, you have believed: Blessed are those who have not seem and yet have believe." **Verses 27-29**. East, west, north and south, all in between Jesus know everything,

A woman of faith struggled abundantly health-wise. A friend didn't fail her, so she kept praising God in her sickness. A writer's song helped her, I believe, from her heart a writer pen entitled "Step Right In." Jesus stepped right in. He used a woman of faith and had compassion on her; invited her into her home, others also. One day I saw the woman of faith in the doctor's office smiling motioning for me to come in. I mention her kindness to help others; she laughed out loud; said her daughters asked her not to take anyone else in. Famously, we laughed out loud at their request, because her daughter had to take off from work to help her get to the doctor's office. Thanks to God her friend was safe with her until He rested her soul; God over life and death. See Jesus' signs wonders, with divine evidences within **verses 30-31** written for us all.

Imagine, we miss the mark thinking we're right. A woman's name wasn't mentioned. "Then the scribes and Pharisees brought to Him the woman caught in adultery. And when they had set her in the midst. They said to Him, Teacher, this woman was caught in adultery in the very act. Now Moses, in the law, commanded us that such should be stoned. But what do you say?" **John 8:3-5**. What would you say? "This they said, testing Him, that they might have something of which to accuse Him. But Jesus stooped down and wrote on the ground with His finger as though He did not hear them." **Verse 6**. I believe, before anyone opened their mouth, Jesus discerned their thoughts miraculously. "So, when they continued asking Him, He raised Himself up and said to them, He who is without sin among you, let him throw a stone at her first. And again,

He stooped down and wrote on the ground. Then those who heard it, being convicted by their conscience went out one by one, beginning with the oldest even to the last." **Verses 7-9a**.

Struggles in this place reveal a time to shout, for it feels so good being in His presence: so. "Jesus was left alone and the woman standing in the midst. When Jesus raised Himself up and saw only the woman. He said to her, woman, where are those accusers of yours? Has no one condemned you? She said, no one LORD. And Jesus said to her, neither do I condemn you; go and sin no more." **Verses 9b-11**. It is a time to shout even struggling the magnificence adoration act of Jesus dwell in my heart to make my case for women; the doors of the church should be open worship God. In which reminds of a hymnal titled, "Magnify the LORD, With Me". "For it pleased the Father that in Him all the fullness should dwell, and by Him, whether things on earth or things in heaven, having made peace through the blood of His cross." **Colossians 1:19-20**.

Isaiah, God's prophet wanted to know these things and he asked questions. "Who has believed our report? And to whom is the power of the LORD revealed? For He shall grow up before Him as a tender plant. And as a root out of a dry ground. He has no form or comeliness; and when we see Him: There is no beauty that we should desire Him." **Isaiah 53:1-2**. I'm glad to speak for myself I believe His report because it is no fake news at all. Yet, struggles begin even for Jesus, none can hide from Him since He sees straight through all of us saved and unsaved. God made the way of escape these things I believe from the depth of my heart I shout out again saying. "But He was wounded for our transgressions he was bruised for, our, inquires, the chastisement of our peace was upon Him; and with His stripes we are healed." **Verse 5**.

For example, a young lady very close to my heart at age sixteen struggled, so she confessed her sins and lived her life by choices. She said enjoyed her way of life very much. East, west, north, and south, my dear readers I received an invitation to come pray for her and I accepted. I prayed the above **verse 5**. I know the Word is absolute. "All we like sheep have gone astray; we have turned everyone to his own way; and the LORD has laid on Him the iniquity of us all." **Verse; See verses 7-11**. As a result, nothing but the Blood of Jesus cleanses us from all our sins by His grace; give God the glory. A song writer penned, "HE Wore a Crown." A another writer penned, "HE IS Only a Prayer Away." East, west, north and south "God IS". "Therefore, I will divide Him a portion with the great, and He shall divide the spoil with the strong. Because He poured out His soul unto death. And He was numbered with the transgressors and He bore the sins of many, and made intercession for the transgressors." **Isaiah 53:12**. "Be of good cheer."

Close to the end of my third chapter a time to shout even in struggles. Ezekiel as a watchman obeyed God. Mordecai helped him the king a charge to keep 'Must Jesus Bare the Cross Alone?' I consider a word from Mount Zion, conspicuously David wrote; "When I consider the work of Your fingers, the moon and the stars, which You have ordained. What is man that you are mindful of him?" **Psalm 8:3-4**. God IS. "You have made him a little lower than the angles, and You have crowned him with glory and honor." **Verse 5**.

"Melchizedek, king of Salem, priest of the Most-High, who met Abraham returning from the Slaughter of the kings and blessed him. To whom also Abraham gave a tenth part of all, first being translated king of righteousness, and the king of Salem, meaning king of peace, without father, without mother, without genealogy, having neither beginning of days nor end of life, but made like the Son of God, remains a priest continually." **Hebrews 7:1-3**. A slaughter is a place where animals are killed and slaughtered. Fast forwarded. I consider Abraham's amazing journey, struggles, and blessings spiritually, physically, mentally and financially, east, west, north, south all in between, Abraham obeyed God. Reminds me in my instruction, Paul wrote, armor used in combat made from metal or in likeness of strong leather to protect saying.

"For we wrestle not against flesh and blood, but against principalities, against powers, against. Rulers, of this darkness of this world, against spiritual wickedness in high places. Wherefore take the armor of God that you may able to withstand in the evil day, having all to stand," **Ephesians 6:12-13**. see faith that works I used in the beginning of my book love that works from God. **Matthew 22:37-39**. "On these two commandments hang all the law and the prophets." **Verse 40**. A sign in my office said hang in their baby Friday is coming; someone borrowed and kept it (smile) a time to shout even in struggles. Moses declared, "LORD: You have been our dwelling place in all generation. Before the mountains were brought forth. Or ever You had formed the world, even from everlasting: You are God." **Psalm 90:1-2**. This amazing **Psalm 90:1-106:48**, a prayer of Moses, a song show oppressors verses submissive God's power works obey Him. "So, teach us to number our days that we may gain a heart of wisdom." **Psalm 90:12**. Stay with Jesus, be bless in Him or Return to God.

Chapter Four

"East, West, North. South and All In Between"

"Give ear, O my people, to my law; incline your ears to the words of my mouth. I will open my mouth in a parable; I will utter dark sayings of old, which we have heard and known, our fathers have told us. We will not hide them from their children. Telling the generation to come the praises of the LORD. And His wonderful works that He has done." **Psalm 78:1-4**. I believe the evidence points us to history lessons to praise God is very informative pass on truth good, verses, bad where ever we live. "He established a testimony for Jacob, and appointed a law in Israel Which He commanded our fathers, that they should make known to their children." **Verse 5**.

Amazingly, it is good to listen certain people my return to His Word daily says. "That the generation to come might know them, the children who would be born. That they may arise and declare them to their children; that they might set their hope on God, and not forget the works of God, but keep His commandments. And may not be like their fathers." **Verses 6-8a**. The author's excellent advice, all generations born and to be born makes it personal we should watch tell our children, facts of life, in which if they play with lose dogs fleas will cling to their skin suck their blood. Asaph, God's chosen leader, one of three temple musicians pleased Him, warned all generations even recorded. "A stubborn and rebellious generation: a generation that did not set its heart aright, and whose spirit was not faithful to God." **Verses 8b** amazingly.

It is wise to complete the chapter and revisit purified facts; I understand the group black lives matter. A certain man taught Sunday school one Sunday who spoke purified truth. He said members of the body of Christ have a calling on all lives. Pastors cannot perform the ministry alone. So, fathers missing from the home points to black lives matter. Struggles began in the home, as well in the house of God for instance, nothing is new under the sun. "The children of Ephraim being armed and carrying bows turned back in that battle. They kept not the covenant of God. And refuse to walk in His law; And forgot His wonders that He had shown them. Marvelous things He did in their sigh of their fathers, in the field of Zoar." **Verses 9-12**. ("Now Hebron was built seven years before Zoar in Egypt." **Numbers 13:22**. Thanks to God to be able to hear, see, feel, smell and taste His greatness, a charge to keep and understand the ways to escape these things says.

"He divided the sea and cause them to pass through; and He made the waters to stand as a heap. In the day time, also he led them with a cloud, and all the night with a light of fire. He cleaved the rocks in the wilderness, and gave them water as out of the great depths. He brought streams also out of the rock, and cause water to run down the rivers." **Verses 13-16**. If these things did not get God's peoples' attention it wasn't because He left them alone incredible its' recorded. "And they sinned yet more against Him by provoking the Most-high in the wilderness. And they tempted God in their hearts by asking meat for their lust. Yea they spoke against God; they said: Can God order a table in the wilderness? **Verses 17-19**. They had to know God fails not.   "As far as the east is from the west, So, far has He removed our transgressions from us. As a father pities his children, So the LORD pities those who fear Him. For He knows our frame: He remembers that we are dust. As for man, his days are like grass; as a flower of the field, so he flourishes." **Psalm 103:12-15**. The sun rises in the east and set in the west; to the north and to the south a compass needlepoint helps me proceed in unfamiliar places. But David said, "For the wind passes over it is gone, and its place never remembers it no more. But the mercy of the LORD from everlasting to everlasting on those who fear Him. And His righteousness to children's children." **Verses 16-17**. These things remind me of Father's Day celebration.

I believe a feast is set aside yearly for fathers east, west, north and south. My youngest grandson was born on Father's Day 2002, his dad was incredible happy; my Bible helps me to see. "And He said, A certain man had two sons: and the younger of them said to his father, Father, give me the potion of goods that falls to me. And he divided to them his living." **Luke 15:11-12**. The father didn't utter a word he acted out of love. "And not many days after the younger son gathered all together, journeyed to a far country, and there, wasted his substance with riotous living. And when he had spent all he had, there arose a mighty famine in that land; and he began to be in want." **Verses 13-14**. A famine in a place lacks food; nothing to be celebrated.

"And he went and joined himself to a citizen of that country; and he sent him into his field to feed swine. And he would gladly have filled his belly with husks that the swine did eat: and no man gave to him." **Verses 15-16.** An old saying says, 'there is no place like home.' "And when he came to himself, he said, how many hired servants of my father have bread enough to spare, and I perish with hunger! I will arise, go to my father, and will say to him, Father, I have sinned against heaven, and before you. And I am not worthier to be called your son: make me as one of your hired servants." **Verses 17-19**. Jesus illustrated parables abundantly clear as crystal:

"And he arose and came to his father. But when he was yet a great way off, his father saw him, and he had compassion, and ran and fell on his neck and kissed him. And the son said unto him, Father, I have sinned against heaven and in your sight, and not worthy to be called your son." **Verses 20-21**. Walking and witnessing within our hometown, east, west, north and south, parables illustrates moral or religious lessons says. "But the father said, bring forth the best robe, and put it on him: and put a ring on his hand, and shoes on his feet: And bring hither the fatted calf, and kill it; and let us eat and be merry." **Verses 22-23**. The son turned back to his father.

Merry means full of mirth, gaiety, laughter gleefully. I believe the father and son knew all lives matter to Jesus so be it. Likewise the father: "For this my son was dead and is alive again; he was lost and is found, they began to be merry. Now his elder son was in the field; And as he came and drew nigh to the house, he heard music and dancing. And he called to the servants, and asked what these things meant." **Verse 24-26**. Thinking of the favor of Jesus delights me since his dad knew his son's shoe size, not a myth; gleefully some socks are made to fit all sizes. Character-wise, a movie resembled the prodigal son to me. A father had two daughters. The dad told his younger daughter to go find her shoes; wear them. She obeyed her dad delighted.

As for, the elder brother envy crept in spread like poison ivy tortures the skin with sores cause inner outer horrific inner outer struggles. "And he said to him, your brother is come; and your father has killed the fatted calf, because he has received him safe and sound. He was angry and would not go in: therefore, his father came out and entreated him." **Verses 27-28**. Consider, my dear readers, I believe the father loved his elder son greatly. However just suppose it was Father's Day; was his elder son happy, sad or bitter? "And he answered said to his father, Lo, these many years I have been serving you: neither transgressed at any time your commandment: and yet you never gave me a kid, that I might make merry with my friends. But as soon as this your son was come, which has devoured your living with harlots, you have killed the fatted calf for him." **Verses 29-30**. Our folks celebrated us; four siblings together on our elder sister's birthday yearly. We approved of it merrily because we had cakes pies and everything nice.

"And he said to him, Son, you are always with me, and all I have is yours. It was right that we should make merry and be glad, for you brother was dead and is alive again, was lost and is found." **Verse 31-32**. It is written says: "Likewise, there will be more joy in heaven over one sinner who repents than ninety-nine just persons who need no repentance." **Luke 15:7**. Even so, consider the evidence for all God's people with a plan and on purpose fast forwarded. "Jesus said, to him, today salvation has come to this house, because he also is a son of Abraham; for the Son of Man has come to seek and to save that which was lost." **19:9-10**. A song writer penned, my sincere request. "LORD Be a Fence All Around Me." The Lord is my help in struggles. I can always trust in God our Father in heaven notable, I know He is greater than inner outer struggles.

Abram inherited Canaan pass it on; "Then Abram went on from Egypt, he and his wife and all that he had, and Lot with him, to the South as far as Bethel. To a place where his tent had been at the beginning, between Bethel and Ai, to the place of the altar which he made there at first." **Genesis 13:1-4a**. Famously, I delight in the absolute true story of since Abram found a place to worship God. "And there Abram called on the name of the LORD. Lot also, who went with Abram, had flocks and herd and tents. Now the land was not able to support them that they may dwell together." **Verses 4b-6**. So, strife and struggles head to toe, these things were repeats.

"And there was a strife between the herdsmen of Abram's livestock. The Canaanites and the Perizzites dwelt in the land. So, Abram said to Lot, please let there be no strife between my herdsmen and your herdsmen, for we are brethren. Is not the whole land before you? Please separate from me. If you take the left, then I will go right. And Lot lifted his eyes and saw all the plain of Jordan, that it was well watered everywhere. **Verses 7-10a.** So, it happened. "Before the LORD destroyed Sodom and Gomorrah: like the garden of the LORD, like the land of Egypt as you go toward Zoar. Then Lot chose for himself all the plain of Jordan, and Lot journeyed east. And they separated from each other." **Verses 10b-11**. See **verses 12-15**.

Fast forwarded, I search purposely for investments as recorded invest in amazing evidences. God's promises to Abram say, "I will make your descendants as the dust of the earth; so, that if a man could number the dust of the earth, then your descendants also could be numbered. Arise, walk in the land through its length and width, for I will give it to you. Then Abram moved his tent, and went and dwelt by the terebinth trees of Mamre, which is Hebron, and built there an alter to the LORD." **Verses 16-18.** Hebron "is a city in the hills of Judah, south of Jerusalem."

Again it happened. My daughter and I walked the length of Broadway to edge of town hoping to spread the

Word with anyone. So we walked to every school stood on the opposite side of the street from the schools passed out tracts with help of a certain teacher who helped us. I believe as believers we are included in the blessings because our faith in God.

I entered a marketplace on the west side of our town; an old friend of our dad was in the place. He shared good news about our father. I wept intensely and wondered if our dad's friend was talking about our dad, the Methodist Preacher, although I did notice a little tenderness he showed to our baby sister. Mindfully aware my twin brother and big sister struggles were huge, he loved using a belt on us! Although we were very young, our dear mother loved us all and showered the four of us tender loving kindness. She didn't put down her husband for his actions to the three of us. We were trained by them because it was supposed to be that way, a faithful husband.

For example, my twin brother and I carried water to the workers in the field at ages four or five years old, and we used a broom handled linked through the ring of the bucket. But by the time we reached the workers the water bucket was empty, so the two of us got a whipping although we didn't cause water to flow from the bucket we needed what would happen to us. We heard the word mean back then, yet back then it was no such law as wrongful child abused from hard labor. When our dad died we heard he was not coming back. My twin and I opened the ice box housed on our front porch ate up his cinnamon rolls; drank pet milk straight from the can. But we dared not touch it while he lived. We heard he wasn't coming back no more to live with us.

As a result, I'm grateful his friend told me many good things about our father being a prominent man. I knew him from having taught at our school Wonder. When he retired, he became a major for years. I recorded in my book, *The Way of Escape These Things*. With Facebook or iPhone or twitter not available back then, I can imagine a picture would have gotten him in trouble with the law. Yet he didn't 'spare the rod.' It may have been his daily number one sermon, as a Methodist preacher of the Gospel. His friend said he returned home from the field, refreshed himself prepared a message preached at a church in Edmondson Arkansas and preached so hard he hit the wall; left his hand print on it. He went home and passed away in his sleep. I was speechless, at a loss for words. We didn't know when he passed away back then; these results I'm grateful.

    Rethinking our dad's struggles, I can't describe my love for him, but it reminded me of an elderly lady made a quilt of many colors that I used miraculously many ways. First, it covers me; reminds me of the blood of Jesus. Secondly, it will last a lifetime. Thirdly, Joseph's dad made him a coat of many colors, **Genesis 37:3**. How awesome is God? Dad's friend knew I was writing my first book. Back then he was very eager to read it and said our dad would've been very pleased with me, since he loved to write sermons to preach them. He said our dad was a good man. I deeply regret our dad's friend did not live to read my book, God rest his soul, rethinking these things.

    Our dear mother said the two had a white Plymouth. I believe a new one, while driving home from church one night, he wrecked their car and a miracle happened. The family could've been sleeping in graves, because the car turned over three times landed straight on its tires again. It took a miracle none of us were hurt and returned home safe. God made a way for us to escape death. He saved us from all harm and danger. My hope in Him reminds today to help others spiritually; struggling or financially as heirs of the promises by faith share His greatness; east, west, north and south according to God's Word. That is our duties by faith in Him.

"After these things, the Word of the LORD came to Abram in a vision saying do not be afraid, I Am your shield, your exceedingly great reward. And Abram said. LORD GOD, what will You give me, seeing I go childless, and the heir of my house is Eliezer Damascus." **Genesis 15:1-2.** Abram, didn't know it but his vision would come to pass. "Then Abram said: Look: You have given me no offspring; indeed, one born in my house is my heir: And behold the word of the LORD came to Him, says this one shall not be your heir. Then He brought him outside and said, look toward heaven, and count the stars if you can number them. And He said them, so shall your descendants be." **Verses 3-5.** It happened God made a covenant with Abram a formal binding agreement between two or more people or groups. Within our Holy Bible it is called the Old Testament and New Testament: Fast forward the power of God faith works in Him saying.

"When Abram was ninety-nine years old, the LORD appeared to Abram and said to him, I AM Almighty God; walk before Me and be blameless. And I will make My covenant between Me and you, and will multiply you exceedingly. Then Abram fell on his face, and God talked to him, saying as for me: My covenant is with you, and you shall be a father of many nations." **Genesis 17:1** A enter thought what is age got to do with God's covenant to Abram? His promises are exceedingly great says. "No longer shall your name be called Abram, but your name shall be called Abraham, for I have made you a father of many nations. I will make you exceedingly fruitful: and I will make nation of you and kings shall come from you.**"**

Verses 2-6. East, west, north, south, the true story cause black lives to be inheritors just believe in God.

"Abraham (Abram) Founder of the Jewish nation an ancestor of Christ his name changed from Abram ("the father of multitudes"); see **Genesis. 11-26; Matthew 1:1, 2.**) Believers commentary: WILLIAMS MACDONALD. One of my favorites; reveals Abraham and Sarah's amazing journeys. Says, "Abraham journeyed from there to the South, and dwelt between Kadesh and stayed at Gerar. Now Abraham said of Sarah his wife: She is my sister. And Abimelech king of Gerar sent and took Sarah. But God came to Abimelect in a dream by night, and said to him, indeed you are a dead man for the woman you have taken is a man's wife." **20:1-3.** The Word says! "But Abimelech had not come near her: And he said LORD will You slay also a righteous nation? Did he not say to me: She is my sister? And she even said herself: He is my brother. In the integrity of my heart and innocence of my hands, I have not done this thing." **Verses 4-5**.

I get it, an old man's tale is humorous even today say, 'when a man marries a wife, she looks so good he could've ate her up: but after the honeymoon, he wished he had ate her up." I smile today, and say maybe his wife felt likewise, smile! Abraham's inner struggles. "God said to him in a dream. Yes, I know you did this in the integrity of your heart; for I also withheld you from sinning against Me: Therefore, I did not let you touch her." **Genesis 20:6.** God see straight through even our thoughts interpret dreams, visions, good or bad. I visited a cousin who lived with her daughter on the north side of town at the age of ninety-four. She buried her husband and their three children. I tested her memory said you look so beautiful, she did. I asked if she knew my name said I know yours' she answered, "you ought to." She scored on me, age didn't matter. His blessings worked for the two of them they had reasons to praise God at her eulogy regardless of age, race or gender we must answer His call whether one live in the east, west, north or south.

God made a charged to Abimelech said. "Now restore the man his wife; for he is a prophet he shall pray for you; and you shall live: And if you will not restore her, know that you shall surely die and all that is yours. Therefore, Abimelech rose early in the morning called his servants, and told all these things in their ears and the men were so afraid." **Verses 7-8**. The fear of the LORD worked in the king 's palace: "And Abimelech called Abraham said to him: What have you done to us? How have I offended you that you have brought on me and my kingdom a great sin? You have done deeds to me that ought not to have been done." **Verse 9.** A question was asked: "Then Abimelech said to Abraham what did you have in view that you have done this thing? And Abraham said I thought surely the fear of God is not in this place, and they will kill me, on, account, of, my wife. But, indeed she is truly my sister. She is the daughter of my father, but not the daughter of my mother: she became my wife." **Genesis 20:10-12.**

More abundantly, the fear of God is to respect Him. "And it came to pass, when God caused him to wander from my father's house, that I said to her, this is your kindness that you should do for me: in every place: wherever we go, say of me, he is my brother. Then Abimelech took sheep, oxen, male and female, and gave them to Abraham: And he restored Sarah his wife to him." **Verses 13-14**. As results, the king made a choice approved by GOD; "And Abimelech said, see, my land is before you; dwell where it pleases you. Then he said to Sarah, Behold, I have given your brother a thousand pieces of silver indeed this vindicates you before all who are with you and everybody. Thus, she was rebuked." **Verse 15**. I consider these things in spirit, mind and heart; Abraham's multi blessings, the king confessions, the key reason to fear and respect Him.

So, my dear readers in the process it happened. "So, Abraham prayed to God: and God healed Abimelech, his wife and his female servants. Then they bore children: For the LORD had closed, up all the wombs of the house of Abimelech because of Sarah, Abraham's wife." **Verses 17-18. This story is** manifested and repeated in other chapters, yet, one thing I know strong winds rise, thunder rolls, lightning flash even so east, west north, south all in between a writer penned a song I believe entitled: "JESUS IS A ROCK IN A WEARY LAND." Moving forward, Jesus teaches us the way and direction to entering the kingdom of heaven consider these things. "They will come from the east and west from the north and south, and sit down in the kingdom of God. And indeed, there are last who will be first, and there will be first last who will first." **Luke 13:29-30**. Struggles continues, review this chapter. I glanced back at **Luke 15** again.

Jesus asked an excellent question that I'm sure His people in the east, west, north and south reread and I copied these things He taught, asked. "What man of you, having a hundred sheep, if he loses one of them, does not leave the ninety-nine in the wilderness, and go after one which is lost until he fines it? And when he has found it, he lays it one his shoulder, rejoicing. And when he comes home, he calls together his friends and neighbors, saying to them, rejoice with me for I have found my sheep which was lost!" **Luke 15:4-6**. Jesus described, I believe that sheep need a shepherd to lead, shield to protect them in likeness of our Good Shepherd protects and shields us. What would you do, will you leave ninety-nine sheep to look for one lost one?

Oftentimes, we forget to examine ourselves, yet, fake news will find us out an old saying is true in that the grass looks greener on the other side. I keep on searching, purposely; an anonymous psalmist penned my heart's desire even in struggles He does not approve of fake news reports so I recopy my thanksgiving song says. "Oh, give thanks to the LORD, for He is good! For His mercy endures forever. Let the redeemed of the LORD say so. Whom He has redeemed from the hand of the enemy. And gathered out of the lands, From the east and from the west, from the north and south. They wandered in the wilderness in a desolate way; they found no city to dwell in." **Psalm 107:1-4**. I said to myself, when Obama was elected president of the United States of America, if I could pass on great and mighty advice to him God is my witness. This song recounts the blessings of righteous living, deliverance and praising Almighty saying.

"Hungry and thirsty, their souls fainted in them. Then they cried out to the LORD in their troubles, and He delivered them out of their distresses. And He led them forth by the right way that they might go to a city from a dwelling place. Oh, that men would give thanks to the LORD for His goodness, and His wonderful works to the children of men!" **Verses 5-8**. One day after church services I stopped by Kroger's pick up a few things a lady talked about her husband loud enough I heard a wonderful testimony. I quoted verse 8 above, the man behind her joined me, I said don't make me shout in this line a white man smiled said go ahead. I always say people of God can have church anyplace, the Spirit of the LORD is infinite, hungry and thirsty they were "For He satisfies the longing soul, and fill the hungry with goodness. Those who sat in darkness and in the shadow of death, bound in affliction and iron. Because they rebelled against the words of God, and despised the counsel of the Most-High God. Therefore, He brought down their hearts with labor: They fell down and there was none to help." **Verses 9-12**.

Who created fake news in the first place? May God help us even in pain, sorrows with dilemmas that reminds me of clouds that hang low almost leveled to the ground will burst in its season. As a reminder for His goodness sake; God said speak to the storm I believed and obeyed Him it passed over to be continued. "Then they cried out to the LORD in their trouble, and he saved them out of their distresses. He brought them out of darkness and the shadow of death and broke their chains in pieces. Oh, that man would give thanks to the LORD for His goodness, and His wonderful works to the children of men!" **Verses 14-15**. So, I witness real news reports that is out today they say when you see something say something so I pass it on reality.

Obama did the eulogy for the slain people in a certain place aired on television; his voice faded away he struggled with pain for the dead and living peoples' who had done great things in that church, turned into darkness. But the people cried to God, Obama sang "Amazing Grace," a light shone when the people joined in praised our LORD, in their pain, struggles, with distresses. So, "He sent His Word, and healed them, and delivered them from their destructions. Oh, that men would give thanks to the LORD for His goodness, and His works to the children of men." **Verses 20-21**. Move on, see **verses 22-37**. The way to escape destruction east, west, north and south says.

"He also blesses them, and they multiplied greatly; and He does not let their cattle decrease. When they were diminished, and brought low through oppression, affliction and sorrow, He pours contempt on princes, and causes them to wander in the wilderness where there is no way:" **Psalm 107:38-40**. Yet, through it all, diminish means to make or become smaller or less important. I always testify God knows us whether we live in the east, west, north of south and to those ones all in between. "Yet He sets the poor on high, far from afflictions, and makes their families like a flock. The righteous see it and rejoice, and all iniquity stops its mouth. Whosoever is wise will observe these things, and they will understand the loving kindness of the LORD." **Verses 41-43**.

Again, it's abundantly clear, the light is shine in the east, west, north and south consider, is to think, and observe it is He who breathed in my spirit to write the book. The same God that caused Jacob greatness and started a family; he dreamed more abundantly notably for whoever to visit or revisit **Genesis 28:10-13**. So, recopy these things says. "Also, your descendants shall be as the dust of the earth: you shall spread abroad to the to the west, and to the east to the north and the south in you, and your seed all families of earth shall be Blessed. Behold, I AM with you, will keep you wherever you go, and will bring you back to this land; for I will not leave you; Until I have done that which I have spoken to you of." **Genesis 28:14-15**.

It is not fake news, black lives matter because being black is all I know, if it wasn't for the Word I would be lost in sin, an old bitter black woman. Black lives matter to God. I'm almost at the end of my book, it is not easy to write a true story; yet He loved someone like Jacob his name means "heel-catcher" **Genesis 25:24** in whom God protects. "Then Jacob awoke from his sleep and said, Surely the LORD is in this place. And I did not know it.

And he was afraid and said: How awesome is this place! This is none other than the house of God. And this is the gate of heaven." **Genesis 28:16-17**. The God of heaven allowed him to sleep then it happened.

"And Jacob rose early in the morning, and took the stone, that he put at his head, set it up as a pillar and poured oil on top of it. And he called this place Bethel; but the name of that city had been previously Luz at the first. And Jacob vowed a vow, saying if Got will be with me, and keep me in this way that I will go and will give me bread to eat: and raiment to put on." **Verses 18-20**. A vow is a promise, or pledge, Jacob said. "So, that I come back to my father's house in peace then the LORD shall be my God. And this stone which I have set as a pillar shall be God's house, and of all that You give me I will surely give a tenth to YOU." **Verse 22**. More abundantly it is written. "So Jacob went on his journey and came to the land of the people of the East." **29:1**.

Moreover, I thought about a man, "And that man was blameless and upright and one that feared God and shunned evil. And seven sons and three daughters were born to him. Also, his possessions were seven thousand sheep, three thousand camels, five hundred yokes of oxen, five hundred female donkeys, and a very large household, so that man was the greatest of all the people of the East." **Verses 1:1b-3**. Job trusted God. His story reaches east, west, north and south, and all in between is deep, a must read to know the way struggles works, a feast began in **verses 4-19**. After his abundant struggles God made a charge to the devil, moreover Job escaped death.

"Then Job arose, tore his robe and shaved his head; and he fell to the ground and worshiped. And said: Naked I came from my mother's womb, and naked shall I return there. The LORD gave, and the LORD has taken away: Blessed be the name of the LORD. In all this Job did not sin nor charge God with wrong." **Verses 20-22**. Yet, Job was tested, tried inside out I'm thankful none was like Job but it happened to every one of us approved by God; see **Chapter 2:113**.

President Obama made history; tested and tried inside out struggles. Again, he was our first black president of the United States of America. A song entitled I believe to be continued, "Signed Sealed and delivered," straight in the Whitehouse eight years; supposedly one term president four years. We, the people of America, voted for him to win the race and he won it. Yet God knew him before he was born with a plan and purpose for such a time as 2009, January 2017. I heard the voice of God said in my kitchen four days before time he was going to be His 44th president born to be the first the black man in history; 'black lives matter' to Him also. Apostle John had a story to tell. The seal is approved to believers. "After these things, I saw four angels standing at the four corners of the earth, holding the four winds, of the earth, that the wind should not blow on the earth, on the sea, or on the green tree. Then I saw another ascending from the east, having the seal of the living God. And he cried with a loud voice to the four angels to whom it was granted to harm the earth and the sea, saying. Do not harm the earth or trees till we have sealed the servants of our GOD on their foreheads." **Revelations 7:1-3**.

Amazingly, see these things Apostle John wrote see the family affair verses 4-8. And I copy "After these things I liked, and behold, a great multitude which no one could number, of all nations, tribes, peoples, and tongues, standing before the throne and before the Lamb, clothed white robes, with palm branches in their hands, crying out with a loud voice saying: Salvation belongs to our God who sits on the throne, and to the Lamb!" **Verses 9-10**. To be continue. "All the angels stood around the throne and the elders and the four living creatures, and fell on their faces before throne and worshiped God, Saying Amen! Blessing and glory and wisdom Thanksgiving and honor and power and might: Be to our God forever and ever Amen." **Verses 11-12.**

Job stuck to his God given speech a "shield of faith" in Him. "The author is unknown 'possible Job.' Some have suggested Solomon, Moses or Elisha.' Job's questions and answers amazingly this chapter, concerned about his character. A magnificence splendid story filled with the finest questions asked. "I have made a covenant with my eyes, why should I look upon a young woman? "For what is the allotment of God from above. And the inheritance of the Almighty from on high? Is it not destruction for the wicked? Does He not see my ways; and count all my steps? If I have walked with falsehood, or if my foot has hastened to deceit." **Job 31:2-5**. Job, asked questions I believe helped him these things says: "Let me be weighed on honest scales. That God may know my integrity." **Verse 6**.

His words favor my doctor's orders; the first thing her nurse says when I enter her office is step on the scales, so she could record my weight. I told her one day that their scales didn't match mine at home we smiled. I obeyed and stepped on the scales. "Job said if my steps have turned from the way, or my heart walked after my eyes, or it any spot adheres to my hands. Then let me sow, and another eat; yes, let my harvest be rooted out. If my heart has been enticed by a woman. Or if I have lurked at my neighbor's door. Then let my wife grind for another. And let others bow down to her." **Verses 7-10**. Job, I believe hated fake news, lies, witch-hunts, far from his heart, he had clean hands says. "For that would-be wicked: yes, it would be iniquity deserving judgment. For that would be a fire that consumes to destruction and would root out all my increase." **Verses 11-12**. Job knew what would stop his increases more abundantly he said.

"If I have despised the cause of my male or female servant when they complained against me. What then shall I do when God rises? When He punishes, how shall I answer Him? Did not He made me in the womb make them? Did not the same One fashion us in the womb? "**Verses 13-15.** Conspicuously, Job debated comfort, and great concern, for others that melts my own heart in likeness of the armor a covering used in combat to protect the body made with heavy metal. More abundantly I long to be faithful to God and others. Since our same God, again, my twin brother and I were formed in my mother's worm, same time abundantly I was the first one out.

Job said. "If I have kept the poor from their desire. Or cause the eyes of the widow to fail. Or eaten my morsel by myself, so the fatherless could not eat. But from my youth I reared him as a father, and from my mother's womb. I guided the widow. If I have seen anyone perish for lack of clothing or any poor man without covering." **Verses 16-19**. In Him, when in doubt, in sorrow, in struggles, and devious thoughts. I consider the great feedback Job said, "If his heart has not blessed me, and if he was not warmed with the fleece of my sheep. If I have raised my hand against the fatherless; when I saw, I had help in the gate; then let my arm fall from my shoulder. Let my arm fall from the socket. For destruction from God is a terror to me. And because of His magnificence I cannot endure." **Verses 20-23**. These magnificence words remind me, the four of us were fatherless children many years GOD's grace by His majesty divine ways we made it.

My desire to obey and, allow Him to use me the rest of my life on earth. For, God teaches His own people the way to escape these things, such as devious thoughts that I hate makes me afraid. Immediately that Sunday Jesus affirmed most urgently a message to mark me, and He did it right on time. Because I boasted ten years as a widow I would never marry again. That Sunday morning our pastor; blessed a young preacher from a big city, attended college in theology to better preach, the Gospel. The twenty-two years preacher preached my own testimony entitled: "Never Say Never." **Luke chapter 1:5**. That fourth Sunday he talked about empty, O LORD I was so excited every time he mentioned Elizabeth debated her case being old and empty I yelled out loud, empty! Someone told on me that! Do not know my true story, so it happened; everything I needed, urgently, a message from God to someone like me. Suddenly, God affirmed my case an old preacher, said he never done better in his life, retired but not tired I penned in my first book a message from the man of God. He passed away a very blessed he obeyed God.

A woman of faith from our former school Wonder said in church, that she would never get married again, I told her never say never; she may miss something good God has for her. She received the message. Jobs words sounded like my words says. "If I have made gold my hope, or said to fine gold you are my confidence. If I have rejoiced because of my wealth was great. And because of my hand had gained much." **Verses 24-25**. East, west, north, and south a writer penned. "There is no secret what God can do." I understand to never say never down deed in my soul, heart and mind looking to Jesus to lead me on, hold me up straight in Him. Even before completing my second book, my confidence in God manifest preciously my faith. It would be immensely great move on a taste, because I feel these things. Job declared it best say.

"If I have observed the sun when it shines, or the moon moving in brightness, so that my heart has been secretly enticed." **Job 31:26**. As for me, I revisit clear powerful revelations, because practice makes permanent, for instant God's majestic words favor a song writer penned entitled, "The Sky Is the Limit." I considered, one night I sat on my porch, I looked up at the sky a star twinkled at me. It was not my imagination. His works in signs and wonders that are seen clear in the sky.

A young missionary struggled exceedingly, an elderly missionary that disliked and envied her. Even so, the two of them confessed Jesus as their Savior privately, and publicly, so right at Christmas I had a plan, and asked the young lady to purchase a lovely Christmas gift since God blessed her with her needs, she was pleased to do it, my plan worked and exceeded envy greatly.

Notably, envy continues yet God show ways to crack nuts even without use of the tool of a nut cracker. For example, Solomon says. "Wisdom strengthens the wise More than ten rulers of a city." **Ecclesiastes 7:19**. So, it be wonderful if young millennials would consider these things. "Also, do not take to heart everything people say, lest you hear your servant cursing you. For many times, also, your own heart has known that even you have cursed others. All this I have proved by wisdom, I said, I will be wise. But it was far from me." **Verses 20-23**. Solomon told it like it was in his elderly years. **See 26-27**. East, west, north, and south his report truly makes excellent sense says. "Which My soul still seeks but I cannot find: One man among a thousand I have found. Truly, this only I have found: That God man made man upright: But have sought out many schemes." **Verses 28-29.** Even so east, west, north and south. I find the way to escape these things within God's Word is good in my taste amazingly Solomon wrote these things just right. "The tongue of the just is as choice silver: the heart of the wicked is little worth. The lips of the righteous feed many: but fools lack wisdom." **Proverbs 10:20-21.**

One day I got lost in Memphis, less than twenty minutes east of my home, but I wasn't focus or paid attention yet God is so very glad I didn't have to waste time He was present all the time. Solomon wrote: "The hope of the righteous will be gladness, but the expectation of the wicked shall perish. The way of the LORD is strength to the upright, but destruction will come to the workers of iniquity." **Verse 28.** Whether Solomon wrote or other writers penned these things, "The righteous will never be moved, but the wicked will not inherit the earth. The mouth of the wickedness brings forth wisdom. But the perverse tongue will be cut off. His lips of the righteous know what is acceptable. The mouth of the wicked is perverse." **Verses 30- 32.**

One day a whirlwind from the north stirred up things while we lived on the Southside. At that time; my three children and I stood in the front door stunned; push hard to close the front door. The wind was so strong it picked up dust, leaves all things in its way. Suddenly a little boy lived close by ran to our door scared as a rabbit. He was struggling very hard the wind almost held him back; immediately God lifted the wind the child escaped the storm at our house.

A woman of faith called me and talk about her past life, in which she allowed heavy burdens inner outer struggles incredible from her youth snatches away her joy.

So, her struggles based on her lack of ability to forgive her past lifestyle; yet all of God's people have a past; the key is to accept it and move forward in the first place. After all, a certain woman struggled during her life. "Jesus said to her, Go, call your husband, and come here, the woman answered and said I have no husband. Jesus said to her You have well said, I have no husband. For you have had five husbands, and the one whom you now have is not her husband. In that you spoke truly." **John 4:16-18.** I shared the true story with her she was satisfied and released from burdens.

Jesus forgives our sins if we confess them to Him see the true story **I John 1:9**, forgiveness of sin comes through Jesus Christ; justified and redeemed by the blood of the Lamb declared us free by faith in Him, I stick to His amazing grace. Paul asked. "Where is boasting then? Is it excluded. By the law? Of works? No but by the law of faith apart from the deeds of the law. Or is He the God of the Jews only? Is He not of the Gentiles? Yes, of the Gentiles also: Seeing it is One God, which shall justify the circumcision by faith, and un-circumcision through faith. Do we then make void the law through faith" Certainly not!" **Romans 3:27-31a**. Therefore, east, west, north and south, the Word is alive God uses ordinary people struggling forgive each other. Paul said, "On the contrary, we establish the law." **Verse 31b**.

Jesus said: "And other sheep I have which are not of this fold; them also I must bring, and they will hear My voice, and there will be one flock and one shepherd." John **10:16.** Jesus, Himself said these bitter sweet words of life. "Therefore, My Father loves Me, because I lay down My life that I may take it up again. No one takes it from Me, but I lay it down of Myself. I have power to lay it down, and I have power to take it again. This command I have received from My Father." **Verses 17-18.** Again, inner outer struggles began. See the entire glory stories saying. "Therefore, there was a division again among the Jews because of these saying. And many of them said, He has a demon and is mad. Why do you listen to Him? Others said, these are not the words of a demon. Can a demon open the eyes of the blind?" verse 19. Jesus is Speaker/Teacher. Fast forwarded **verses 20-42.** Believer, know the Father, Son, Holy Spirit works for life.

    Remember, God revealed Ezekiel to me again, as a reminder to see the way God worked years ago show His divine power to Ezekiel he testified. "The hand of the LORD came upon me and brought me out in the Spirit of the LORD, set me down in the valley; and it was full of bones. Then He caused me to pass by them all around, and behold, there were very many in the opened valley. And lo they were very dry." **Ezekiel 37:1-2.** Ezekiel faced tough questions "And He said to me, Son of man can these bones live? So, I answered, O LORD GOD You know. Again, He said to me Prophesy, to these bones, and say to them, O ye dry bones hear the Word of the LORD! Thus, says the LORD God to these bones: Behold I will cause breath to enter you, and you shall live." **Verses 3-5.** Down deep in my soul one of my favorite revelations show us the way to escape these things I call walking dead bones and use God's Word I say.

    We can't breathe without God: it is written says, "I will lay sinews on you and will bring flesh upon you, and cover you with skin put breath in you; and you shall live. And you shall know that I AM God." **Verse 6.** The case for us for all generations revealed the way God cover our flesh. Ezekiel said. "So, I prophesied as He commanded me, and the breath came into them, and they lived, and stood upon their feet, an exceeding great army. Then He said to me:

Son of man, these bones are the whole house of Israel: behold, they say: Our bones are dried, and our hope is lost: we are cut off for our parts." **Verses 10-11**. God used Ezekiel to speak out as recorded he wrote. "Therefore, prophesy and say to them, Thus, said the LORD God; Behold, O my people, I will open your graves, and cause you to come up out of your graves, and bring you into the land of Israel." **Verse 12-13**. I cannot count the times God introduced Himself in His Word saying, "Then you shall know that I AM the LORD, when I have opened your graves, O my people, and brought you up out of the graves. I will put My Spirit in you, and you shall live, and I will place you in your own land. Then shall you know that I the LORD, have spoken it, and performed it said the LORD." **Verses 13-14**. A reunion is good, the Math is excellent show.

One King, one Kingdom says, "Again the Word of the LORD came to me, saying. As for you, son of man, take a stick for yourself and write on it: For Judah and for her children of Israel, his companions. Then take another stick and write on it. For Joseph, the stick of Ephraim, and for all the house of Israel, his companions. Then join them one to another into one stick, and they will become one in your hand," **Verses 15-17**. I pen because I believe these words were heard east, west, north, and south because the people of God got the message we continue to study today. It is amazing I stick to His Word. And the people used a real stick.

"And when the children of your people speak to you, saying, will you not show what you mean by these? Say to them, Thus, said the LORD God: Surely, I will take the stick of Joseph, which is in the hand of Ephraim, and the tribes of Israel, his companions; and I will join them with it, the stick of Judah, and make them one stick, and they will be one stick in My hand. **Verses 18-19**. God solves the problems. Ezekiel passed it on: "And the sticks on which you write will be in your hand before your eyes. Then say to them thus says the LORD God. Surely, I will take the children from among the nations, wherever they have gone, and will gather them from every side and bring them into their own land." **Verses 20-21**. I believe, east, west, north and south his report opened the way to escape doubts that could cause beating rapid heart attacks says.

"And I will make them one nation in the land, on the mountains of Israel; and one king shall be king over them all; they shall no longer be two nations, nor shall they ever be divided into two kingdoms again. They shall not defile themselves anymore with their idols nor with their detestable things, nor with their transgressions." **Verses 22.** But I will deliver from their dwelling place in which they have sinned, and cleanse them. Then they shall be my people, and I will be their God." **Verses 22-23a**. Detestable things are wickedness filled with idol worship in land that was full of these things, but God said. "David My servant shall be king over them, and they shall have one Shepherd; they shall also walk in My judgments and observe My statures, and do them. Then they shall dwell in the land that I have given to Jacob My servant, where your fathers dwelt; and they shall dwell there, they, their children, and their children's children, forever, And My servant shall be their prince forever." **Verse 24-25**. East, west, north and south. Then it happened I find great feedback there are inner outer struggles but God is greater He said.

"Moreover, I will make a new covenant of peace with them, and it shall be an everlasting covenant with them: I will establish them and multiply them, and it shall be set My sanctuary in their midst forevermore. My tabernacle also shall be with them; indeed, I will be their

God, and they shall be my people." **Verse 26-27**. As for me, I continue to worship God who made the way of escape these things, for His people. East, west, north, south, and all in between He knows the struggles are a part of life yet His covenant is everlasting the weeping prophet of God Jeremiah. His lifestyle was a massage that could've kept him alone, and lonely; but God was with him. He said, "The Word of the LORD also came to me, saying, you shall not take a wife, nor shall you have sons or daughters who are born in this place, For, thus says the LORD concerning their mothers who bore them and their fathers who begot them in this land." **Jeremiah 16:1-3**.

God's plans for his weeping prophet declared His reasons not Jeremiah's who was called by God "Then the Word of God came to me saying. Before I formed you in the womb I knew you." **1:5 see verses 10**. What a plan and gruesome purpose Jeremiah faced born to suffer it is written. "They shall die a gruesome, deaths; they shall not be lamented nor shall they be buried, but they shall be like refuse on the face of the earth. They shall be consumed by the sword and famine, and their corpses shall be meat for the birds of heaven, and for the beasts of the field. But the LORD said, "Do not enter the house of mourning, nor go to lament, or bemoan them. For God have taken away My peace from this people, says the LORD, loving-kindness and mercies. Both the great and the small shall die in this land." **Verses 4-5**. Darkness was manifested through the land, I believe, on the east, west, north, south side of this land the same place.

"Both the great and the small shall die in the land. They shall not be buried; neither shall men lament for them, cut themselves, nor make themselves balm for them." **Verses 6.** See **verses 7-11**; **verses 12and 13** summarizes, His people reacted to our amazing God IS! Saying. And you have done worse than your father, for behold, each one dictates of his own evil heart, so that no one listens to Me. Therefore, I will cast you out of this land that you do not know, neither you nor your fathers; and you have served other gods day and night, where I will not show you favor." God watches, He reveals the way to restore Israel says, "Therefore, behold, the days, ARE coming says the LORD, that it shall no more be said: The LORD lives who brought up the children of Israel from the land of Egypt. But, the LORD lives who brought up the children of Israel from the land of the north and from all the lands where He had driven them, for I will bring them back to their land which I gave to their fathers." **Verses 14-15.**

Therefore, a taste of light after the storms passed away Jeremiah wrote "Remember, my affliction and roaming, the wormwood and the gall. My soul still remembers and sinks within me. This I recall to my mind. Therefore, I have hope. Through the LORD'S mercies we are not consumed, because His compassions fail not. They are new every morning Great is Your faithfulness." **Lamentations 3:20-24.** Consider Jeremiah kept hope alive and penned: "The LORD is good to those who wait for Him. To the soul who seeks Him. It is good that one should hope and wait quietly for the salvation of the LORD." **Verses 25-26.**

A glimpse back, listening to the elders testify, God is on our side acknowledging the way He loves His people I have many reasons to agree with them. A friend, and former classmate of our school Wonder. Her dad gave us a trip to the windy city Chicago after high school graduation. And, struggles began on our way home I fell fast asleep driving her dad's and suddenly, God woke me up on the bank of the river gazed as black waters it may have been near midnight. My friend woke up she asked, where were we? Again, I was abundantly speechless with fear. We looked at the big black lake flow back and forth like the waters were waiting restless for us to join the black flowing lake. God is my witness it wasn't a dream He made away for us to escape death on our way to our hometown West Memphis Arkansas, the God of heaven, earth and seas holds the east, west, north and south in His hand canceled a death notice and kept us abundantly alive. Nothing but the purified truth so help God IS our shield of protection asleep or awake.

      Even in my youth He worked strange blessings, but I was afraid to tell anyone at age eleven years old. Rethinking, who would believe that I was bashful for years? But God reminded me of the little children in our neighborhood whose mom and dad passed away, it wasn't a dream. I combed their hair daily; helped prepared them for school every morning. On a certain day, I ran into one in the marketplace, I realize in awe we were both senior citizens, and I asked, if she remembered I helped them dressed them for school? To my amazement, she said yes. I felt the joy of the LORD, and I rejoiced in Him because even back then I loved helping people, that is my goal even today. So, one day I met the other sister in the marketplace asked her the same thing. She remembered I was only three years older than she was what a blessing I was startled.

      God refreshed my memory, because Jesus said how could I write a book without words from the "Sermon on the Mount?" Again, I was at a loss for words. So, when He opened my mouth I said, LORD You, instructed me to write the book; and said God has a great sense of humor even so, He said write the book. Again, God revealed to me said don't worry about the publisher. Even today, I still do not know exactly what God meant, but I have a taste of knowledge that makes it plain, the Spirit is indeed teaching me it's not about me, but the purified Word is key.

So, it happened, again I couldn't wait to share amazingly with whosoever would listen to me. So, today, I know the reason God allowed a certain pastor one of His chosen one's to purposely say to me, you have four books to pen, I believed him, east, west, north and south because He, the Spirit breathed my titles within my spirit. As results, as I listen to the Spirit of God in my ear, to tell me what to write, and delete, is one of the best things that happened to someone like me alone, but not alone. There is no way for me to express God's, love, grace, mercy, strengthens me with joy, peace, comfort, and hope, purposely in Him, through Him, because of Him I accept, the gift by Him it happened. I continue to write obey Him even so, I'm not worthy, Jesus said.

"Blessed are the poor in spirit: For theirs in the kingdom of heaven. Blessed are they that mourn: for they shall be comforted. Blessed are the meek: For they shall inherit the earth. Blessed are they that do hunger and thirst after righteousness: for they shall be filled; Blessed are the merciful for they shall obtain mercy." **Matthew 5:3-7**. God's majestic infinite revelations declares: "Blessed are the pure in heart: For they shall see God. Blessed are the peacemakers: For they shall be called the children of God. Blessed are they which are persecuted for righteousness' sake: For theirs is the kingdom of heaven." **Verses 8-10**.

He's ever present, east, west, north, south and all in between. I recall God kept me safe in the process of time my eyes failed to blink, my mouth twisted slightly. I looked in the mirror at work God provided a witness in place. I asked if she noticed anything strange with my mouth. She glanced at my face didn't see what I saw. Suddenly I left work, returned home called for an appointment with my doctor, but his nurse said he was booked until Friday it was Tuesday. I made an appointment for Friday I waited and prayed for healing. I faced with the doctor he took one look asked why I didn't go to the emergency room that Tuesday. I responded they would have referred me back to the doctor, he said I could've had a stroke that thought didn't enter my mind at all instead today inspiringly I thought even in struggles, the voice of God substance is faith in Him for He is famously our Healer.

David, the anointed of God, whether good or hard times, like running from Saul, or in times of prosperity or struggling with his enemies; he remembered God said. "Blessed be the LORD my strength, which teaches my hands to war, and my fingers to fight: My goodness and my fortress, my high tower, and my deliver; my shield, in whom I trust who subdued my people under me. LORD what is man that You take knowledge of him?" **Psalm 144:1-3**. David asked questions, I believe and answered them for the people of God says, "Man is like a breath: His days are like a passing shadow." See **verse 5-14.** The last verse says, "Happy are the people who are in such a state; Happy are the people whose God is the LORD. The way of escape these things.

Although we struggle, as did God's servants in all generations, whenever I looked beyond self it is good for me to acknowledge in my heart, I stick to, we're saved by the blood of Jesus, by God's grace I confess our Savior He is LORD. Paul won his debates struggling, but he penned purified truths, faced reality say: "But now, it is no longer I who do it, **Romans 7:17a**. Moving on he said, "I find then a law, that when I would do good, evil is present with me. For I delight in the law of God after the inward man: But I see another law in my members, warring against the law of my mind, and bringing into captivity to the law of sin which is in my members" **Romans 7:21-23.** Awesomely, Paul wrote what he found out, as do I, awed-struck amazingly in many struggles throughout his lifetime he had great times in the LORD, in which I believe his confessions says. "O wretched man that I am! Who shall deliver me from the body of this death?" **Verse 24**. These things capture my utmost attention every time I revisit this "breaking news report." "I thank God through Jesus Christ our LORD. So then with the mind I myself serve the law of God: But with the flesh the law of sin." **Verse 25**.

    A song I believe David dedicated a thanksgiving prayer says. "You have turned my mourning into dancing: You have put off my sackcloth and clothe me with gladness: To the end that my glory may sing praise to You and not be silent: O LORD I will give thanks to you forever." **Verses 11-12**. David celebrated sweet music songs of praises, my dear readers, take a peep back, **See Psalm 30:1-10**. Close to the end of my book a summary having obtained favor from God David had favor God blessed many people, his son Solomon was abundantly blessed says "Thus Solomon's wisdom excelled the wisdom of all men of the East and all the wisdom of Egypt, for, he was wiser than all men." **I Kings 4:30-31a**. Moses wrote, "You shall be Holy for I AM holy." **Lev 19:2**. Jeremiah says. "Call unto Me and I will answer you and show you great and mighty things you do not know." **Verse 33:3**. A song writer wrote: Every Day is Thanksgiving:"

    "And Adam called his wife Eve, because she was the mother of all living things." **Genesis 3:20**. In the east, west, north south, and all in between. Amen. Even in amazing struggles, Sarah had a charge to keep, "Then the LORD said to Abraham Why Sarah? **See Gen. 18:13a**. "Is anything too hard for the LORD.? At the appointed time Sarah shall have a son." **Verse 14**.

A young man prayed, my dear readers, a prominent prayer to the God of his silent years remember my first chapter. "You have not given the weary water to drink. And you have withheld bread from the hungry, But the mighty man possessed the land, And the honorable man dwelt in it. You have sent widows empty." **Job 22:7-9**. I used 'a father pities his children.' "Black Lives Matter." Even to the God of his silent years to rest in Him. I offer give thanks to God pray, and commune with Him and used properly I **Corinthians 11:24-26**. So be it.

David's confession, and Nathan's parable constantly intensifies my spirit saying: "The LORD sent Nathan to David. And he came to him; there were two men in one city, one rich and the other poor. The rich man had exceedingly many flocks and herbs. But the poor man had nothing, except one ewe lamb which he had bought and nourished." **II Samuel 12:1-3a.** A poor man verses a rich man guest who was in the house? I believe struggling inside out saying "And it grew up together with his children. It ate of his own food and drank and drink from his own cup and lay in his bosom: and it was like a daughter to him." **Verse 3b**.

Guest who rested on his journey? "And a traveler came to the rich man, who refused to take from his own flock and from his own herd to prepare one for the wayfaring man who had come to him. But he took the poor man's lamb and prepared it for the man who had come to him." **Verse 4**. Now the parable reveals a chosen favorable man of God heard about it. "So, David's anger was greatly aroused against the man, and he said to Nathan, As the

LORD lives, the man who had done this shall surely die! And he shall restore fourfold for the lamb, because he had no pity. Then Nathan said to David, You are the man." **Verses 5-7a**. Beware, struggles creep in.

God of Israel: I anointed you king over Israel, and delivered you from the hand of Saul. I gave you your master's house and your master's wives into your keeping, and gave you the house of Israel and Judah. And if that had been too little, I also would have given you much more!" **Verses 7b-8**. A question was asked: "Why have you despised the commandant of the LORD to do evil in his sight? You have killed Uriah the Hittite with the sword; you have taken his wife to be your wife, and have killed the sword of the people of Ammon." **Verse 9; see verses 10-12**.

David's sins, as God would have it, were opened to the public in his own family. He confessed. "So, David said to Nathan, I have sinned against the LORD. And Nathan said to David I have put away your sin; you shall not die; however, because of the deed you have great occasion to the enemies of the LORD to blaspheme, the child shall surely die. Then Nathan departed to his house." **Verses13-15a**. It came to pass. "And the LORD struck the child that Uriah's wife bore to David, and it became ill. David pleaded with God for the child, and he fasted and went in and lay all night on the ground. So, the elders of his house arose and went to him, to rise from the ground, but he would not, nor, did, he eat-food with them." **Verses 15b-17**. Struggles will show up anytime at home or outside, whether we live east, west, north, south, all in between on earth. We reap what we sow my dearest readers Jesus wins His case. Seven days mean completion. "Then on the seventh day, it came to pass that the child died. And the servants of David were afraid to tell him that the child was dead. For they said, indeed while the child was alive we spoke to him, and he would not heed our voice. How can we tell him that the child is dead?" He may do some harm!" **Verses 18**. So, I consider a charge to keep; sin must be a confession repent turn from it ask God to forgive us any place and time.

"When David saw, his servants were whispering, David perceived that the child was dead. So, David arose from the ground, washed and anointed himself and changes his clothes: and went into the house of the LORD and worshiped. Then He went to his own house; and he requested, they set food before him, and he ate it." **Verses 19-20**. I leaped up; worshiped God; anointed myself and bowed on my knees prayed to Him. "And he said, while the child was alive, I fasted and wept; for I said, who can tell whether the LORD will be gracious to me that the child may live? But now he is dead; why should I fast? Can I bring him back again? I shall go to him but he shall not return to me." **Verses 21-22**. Blessings verses struggles; he knew right from wrong.

"Then David comforted Bathsheba his wife, and went in to her and lay with her. So, she bore a son, and he called his name Solomon. Now the LORD loved him. And He sent word by the hand of Nathan the prophet: So, he called his name Jedidiah, because of the LORD." **Verses 23-24**. East, west, north, south, and all in between, I said to myself, no wonder our grandfather loved to talk about a young man called Jedidiah. Over in the Book of Acts, I will take you to the place that David made a speech blows my mind, opened my heart comfort me, "No Greater Love."

"For David speaks concerning Him, I foresaw the LORD always before my face, for He in on right hand, that I should not be moved; therefore, my heart did rejoice, and my tongue was glad, moreover my flesh shall rest in hope: Because You will not leave my soul in hell, neither will You suffer your holy one to see **Acts 2:25-27.** A glance back these things continue to manifest a family affair these days I truly believe, good or bad, two-way paths are written; "Now these are the last words of David. Thus, says David the son of Jesse. Thus, says the man raised up on high, the anointed of God of Jacob. And the Sweet Psalmist of Israel." **II Samuel 23:1.**

David testified, I know for sure, wonders, acts and miracles works he confessed it, "The Spirit of the LORD Spoke by me, and His word was on my tongue, the God of Israel said, the Rock of Israel Spoke to me: He who rules over men must be just, ruling in the fear of God, and he shall be like the light of the morning when the sun rises a morning without clouds." **Verses 2-4.** I walked outside one morning there were no clouds in the sky I turned toward, the east, the sunrises, then west, north and south, my doctor said the sun provides the best vitamin D that I needed. Avoid being sun burnt, a natural act, God works miracles, a family affair from Him

Even so, the struggles of the black man past and present, the door is opened; just walk right in. I see many prominent men of color standing up for Jesus, we have seen the story.

"He rules over men must be just," I believe even east, west, north, south and all in between. The case is open wide "black lives matters", whosoever is willing lead our young people regardless of where they live? Obama's God given vision he talked about it passed on: "Am I my brother's keeper? Hillary said she would make Healthcare better an experience saved by grace woman of God, I believe struggles made her stronger walking her dog in the woods. Even so, Hillary reminds me of a wise woman named is mentioned in a key versed says: "Then David said to Abigail: Blessed is the LORD GOD of Israel, who sent you this day to meet me! And blessed is your advice and blessed are you, because you have kept me this day from coming to bloodshed and from avenging myself with my own hand." **I Samuel 25:32-33**.

Remember, God said to Jonah: "And should not I pity Nineveh, that great city, in which are more than one hundred twenty thousand persons who cannot discern between their right hand and their left hand and much life stock?" Jonah 4:11. Healthcare is a struggle for many people, inner outward, like the pilot said in sky in the air plane pray God is listening. I believe God said the Affordable HealthCare will prosper; we the people get ready, watch and pray. **James 5:16; Psalm 23:1-6.**

GOD IS!

MAY GOD ALWAYS BLESS AMERICA EAST, WEST, NORTH AND SOUTH.

From the Author

Someone once mentioned royal blue to me. That color stuck with me. Royal to me means prestige; of a certain character. It also reminds me of God. So now when I think of royalty and royal blue, I think of God's grace and loving mercy.

"When you walk with God, you walk in Royalty"
Jeweline R. Andrews